LETTERHEADS

Gone Digital

Edited by
David E. Carter

Book Design & Captions by
Suzanna M.W. Brown

Letterheads Gone Digital

First published 1998 by Hearst Books International
1350 Avenue of the Americas
New York, NY 10019

ISBN: 0-688-16476-5

Distributed in the U.S. and Canada by
Watson-Guptill Publications
1515 Broadway
New York, NY 10036
Tel: (800) 451-1741
(732) 363-4511 in NJ, AK, HI
Fax: (732) 363-0338

ISBN: 0-8230-6624-X

Distributed throughout the rest of the world by
Hearst Books International
1350 Avenue of the Americas
New York, NY 10019
Fax: (212) 261-6795

First published in Germany by
Nippan
Nippon Shuppan Ilanbai
Deutshland GmbH
D-40549 Dusseldorf
Telephone: (0211) 504 8089
Fax:: (0211) 504 9326

ISBN: 3-931884-40-6

Printed in Hong Kong by Everbest Printing Company
through Four Colour Imports, Louisville, Kentucky.

Table of **Contents**

One of the most difficult and time-consuming aspects of creating camera-ready artwork before the computer era was cutting overlays of rubylith or amberlith. Each color needed its own overlay. Each percentage of each color needed its own overlay. Each shape, in all its intricacy, needed to be cut by hand from the overlay. One little slip of the X-acto...and you had to start ALL OVER AGAIN.

Now, with a point and click, separations print out directly and exactly to film.

creative firm: **SAYLES GRAPHIC DESIGN**
designer: **John Sayles**
client: **Goodwin Tucker Group**

Cutting shapes on rubylith meant exact precision so touching colors wouldn't overlap and create an unwanted line.

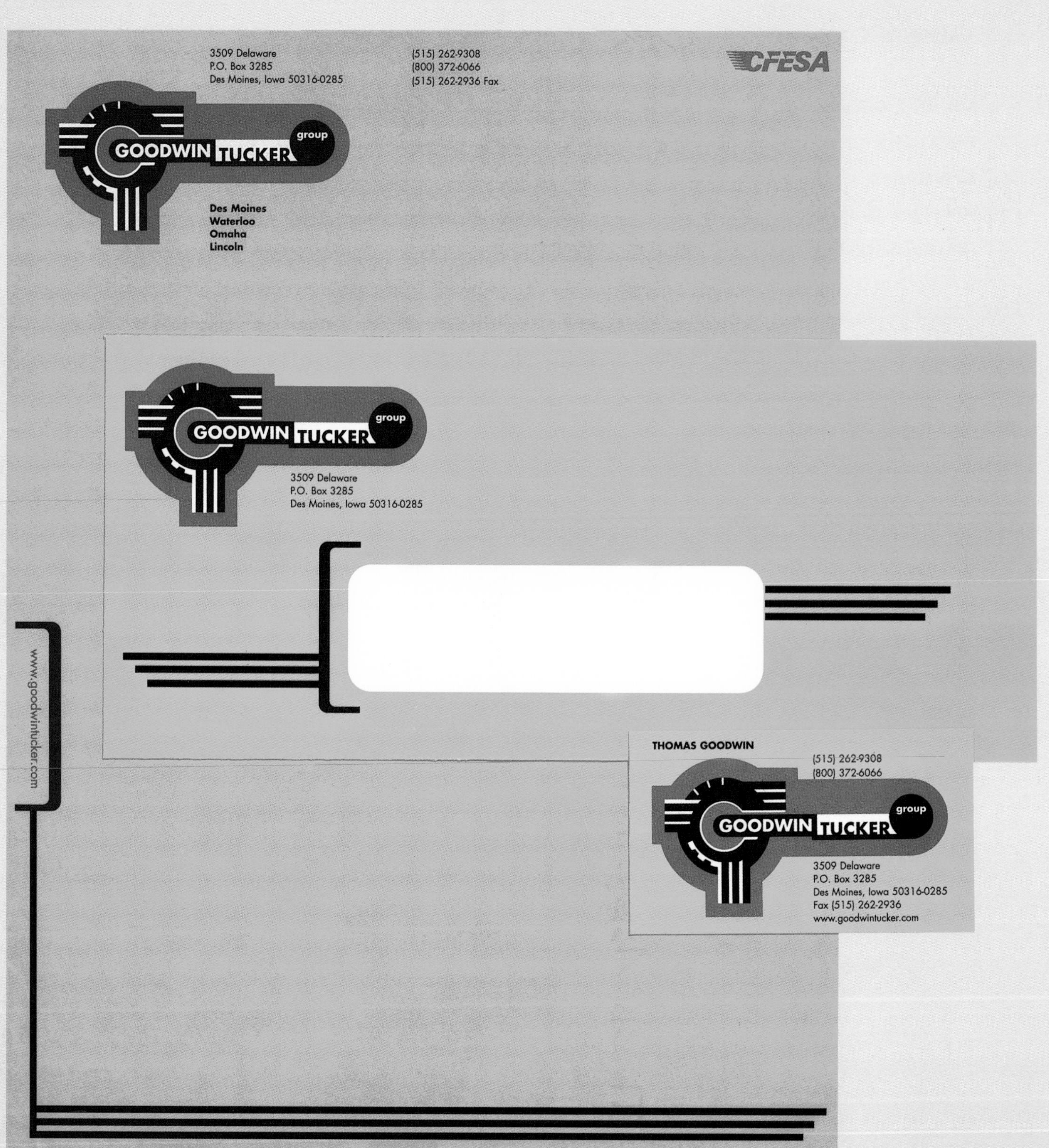

The stationeries on these two and the next several pages are good examples of techniques which are much simpler to execute with the aid of Macintosh than without: touching colors, reversed type, percentages of colors, detailed images, several spot colors used in one design, and light colors "over" dark colors.

creative firm: **FUSE, INC.**
designer: **Russell Pierce**
client: **Fuse, Inc.**

This example of "overlapping" screens would have been made difficult by just trying to remember what piece was supposed to be which screen.

creative firm: **HANDLER DESIGN GROUP, INC.**
designers: **Bruce Handler, Jon Voss**
client: **Handler Design Group, Inc.**

Not only would the division of the "H" have to be exactly cut on this logo, the soft-edge of the shadow simply couldn't be cut.

The Handler Design Group, Inc.

Strategic Marketing Communications & Design

17 Ralph Avenue
White Plains, NY 10606
914 997 7592
914 997 6467 fax
Design8@IX.netcom.com

The Handler Design Group, Inc.

Strategic Marketing Communications & Design

17 Ralph Avenue
White Plains, NY 10606

The Handler Design Group, Inc.

Strategic Marketing Communications & Design

17 Ralph Avenue
White Plains, NY 10606
914 997 7592
914 997 6467 fax
Design8@IX.netcom.com

Bruce Handler

creative firm: MORTENSEN DESIGN
designers: Gordon Mortensen, Diana Kauzlarich
client: Mortensen Design

Cutting all these curving, touching letters would have been murder.

D E S I G N

D E S I G N

mor ten sen

D E S I G N

Gordon Mortensen
Owner/Principal Designer
Mortensen Design
416 Bush Street
Mountain View, CA 94041
Email: gmort@opni.com

P. 650 988 0946 • F 650 988 0926

Mortensen Design 416 Bush Street Mountain View, CA 94041-2106 P. 650.988.0946 F. 650.988.0926

creative firm: **C3 INCORPORATED**
designer: **Randall Hensley**
client: **C3 Incorporated**

How would you like to trim out this "incorporated" from your overlay for green?

C 3
INCORPORATED
419 Park Avenue South 5th Floor
New York New York 10016
tel > 212.252.0550 fax > 212.252.1180 www > c3inc.com

C 3
INCORPORATED
419 Park Avenue South 5th Floor
New York New York 10016

C 3
INCORPORATED
419 Park Avenue South 5th Floor
New York New York 10016
tel > 212.252.0550 fax > 212.252.1180
www > c3inc.com

SYLVIA CHU
senior designer schu@c3inc.com

> concepts
> consulting
> communications

creative firm: **KRUEGER WRIGHT DESIGN**
designer: **Bob Tema**
client: **Myers Thompson PA**

Knocking out the type on this logo would have been easy compared to trying to achieve the rough edge.

Myers Thompson
Professional Association

603 Colwell Building
123 North 3rd Street
Minneapolis, MN
55401-1629

Phone **612.349.3030**
Fax 612.349.3033

Immigration &
Nationality Law

Myers Thompson
Professional Association

603 Colwell Building
123 North 3rd Street
Minneapolis, MN
55401-1629

creative firm: **GROUP C DESIGN**
designer: **Benjamin Franklin**
client: **Group C Design**

Achieving this logo wouldn't have been impossible - if overprinting was utilized. The **perfect** circle would only need to be cut once.

creative firm: ESDALE ASSOCIATES, INC.
designers: Susan Esdale, Ilse Krause
client: Just Cause

If the edges of these colored boxes overlapped or spacing occurred between them, you could always tell the client it was the printer's fault!

858 West Armitage #214
Chicago Illinois 60614
telephone 312 458 9448
e-mail justcause@pobox.com
http://www.pobox.com/~justcause

Just Fundraisers for Cancer Causes

JustCause

858 West Armitage #214
Chicago Illinois 60614

JustCause

JustCause

creative firm: GR8
designers: Morton Jackson, Charles Gates
client: Gr8

Only a two-color printing job, but three layers of amberlith would be needed because one of the colors is printed in a percentage.

809 CATHEDRAL ST. BALTIMORE, MD 21201

telephone 410 837-3234

facsimile 410 837-6525

www.browncapital.com

creative firm: AAD
designers: Carl F. Schaffer, Michael E. Steveson
client: AAD

Cutting an overlay for the uneven edges of either the yellow or blue boxes could be done at will, but don't forget the knockout for type.

Michael E. Steveson AIA **Carl F. Schaffer** AIA

aad

15425 North Greenway-Hayden Loop
Scottsdale Arizona 85260

aad

interiors architecture identity

interiors architecture identity

Carl F. Schaffer AIA
Principal

aad

602.998.4200 x.201
15425 N. Greenway-Hayden Loop
Scottsdale Arizona 85260
602.998.7643/fax
cschaffer@aadifa.com

15425 North Greenway-Hayden Loop Scottsdale Arizona 85260 602.998.4200 602.998.7223/fax www.aadifa.com

interiors architecture identity

creative firm: **A-HILL DESIGN**
designer: **Sandy Hill**
client: **Form + Function**

This logo appears very unstructured, but line uniformity is constant. The outlines of the logo shapes would have been very difficult to manage.

form+function

1807 SECOND STREET, #9
SANTA FE, NEW MEXICO 87505

form+function

TRISH GONZALES

1807 SECOND STREET, #9
SANTA FE, NEW MEXICO 87505
PHONE/FAX 505/ 820-7872
PHONE/FAX 800/ 264-0057

form+function

328 SOUTH GUADALUPE STREET
SANTA FE, NEW MEXICO 87501

PHONE 505/ 984-8226
FAX 505/ 984-2140

creative firm: ENVIRONMENTAL COMMUNICATIONS ASSOCIATES, INC.
designers: Traci Schalow, A.J Grant
client: CDR

Here are two squiggly lines in accordance with color blocks and negative type. Keeping all those "overlaps" straight would take some real study.

Collaborative Decision Resources

CDR Associates • 100 Arapahoe Ave. • Suite 12 • Boulder, CO 80302

Collaborative Decision Resources

CDR Associates

100 Arapahoe Ave. Suite 12 • Boulder, CO 80302
Ph: 303-442-7367 • Fax: 303-442-7442
http:\\www.mediate.org • cdr@mediate.org

CDR Associates • 100 Arapahoe Ave. Suite 12 • Boulder, CO 80302 • Ph: 303-442-7367 • Fx: 303-442-7442 • http:\\www.mediate.org
Mediation • Environmental/Public Policy Issues • Workplace Conflicts • Custom Dispute Resolution Systems • Training

creative firm: THE BENCHMARK GROUP
designers: Chris Forsythe, Ray Gedeon
client: Millennia III, Inc.

Each different percentage of blue in the circles and squares of the logo would have to be cut from individual overlays.

creative firm: **EM DASH DESIGN**
designer: **Erika K. Maxwell**
client: **Geferan Systems**

It's possible to print dark colors over lighter ones, but the moon and stars would still have to be cut out of the rubylith for blue ink.

Geferan Systems

CLEAR THINKING IN CAM AUTOMATION

Geferan Systems

Post Office Box 410
Richmond, VA 23218

Geferan Systems

Shane Miller
President

Post Office Box 410
Richmond, VA 23218
(804.359.7567
804.338.4111
shanem@netcom.com

CLEAR THINKING IN CAM AUTOMATION

Post Office Box 410 • Richmond, VA 23218
(804.359.7567 • 804.338.4111
email: shanem@netcom.com

creative firm: **V N O DESIGN**
designer: **Jim Vienneau**
client: **A Matter of Taste**

These shapes, though simple, would need to be masterfully executed so they wouldn't gap or overlap.

creative firm: MICHAEL LEE ADVERTISING & DESIGN, INC.
designers: Michael Lee, Debby Stasinopoulou
client: SF Consulting

The black lines in these shapes would allow for less than perfect cuts, but so many little shapes would still be tedious.

HARDWARE. SOFTWARE. NETWORKING. MAKING THE PIECES FIT.

SF·CONSULTING 1550 Industrial Park Road, Nederland, Texas 77627-3118

HARDWARE
SOFTWARE
NETWORKING
MAKING THE PIECES FIT.

Stafford Fields

SF·CONSULTING
1550 Industrial Park Road
Nederland, Texas 77627-3118
409 721-5566 Fax 409 726-8020

SF·CONSULTING

Maintenance & Support, Network Implementation, System Hardware 1550 Industrial Park Road, Nederland, Texas 77627-3118 409 721-5566 Fax 409 726-8020

creative firm: **DISANTO DESIGN**
designer: **Roseanne DiSanto**
client: **Barton Productions**

Remember—each color and each percentage of a color needed its own overlay.

creative firm: **McGAUGHY DESIGN**
designer: **Malcolm McGaughy**
client: **Decision Support Search Co.**

Fine lines and little letters still needed to be cut by hand.

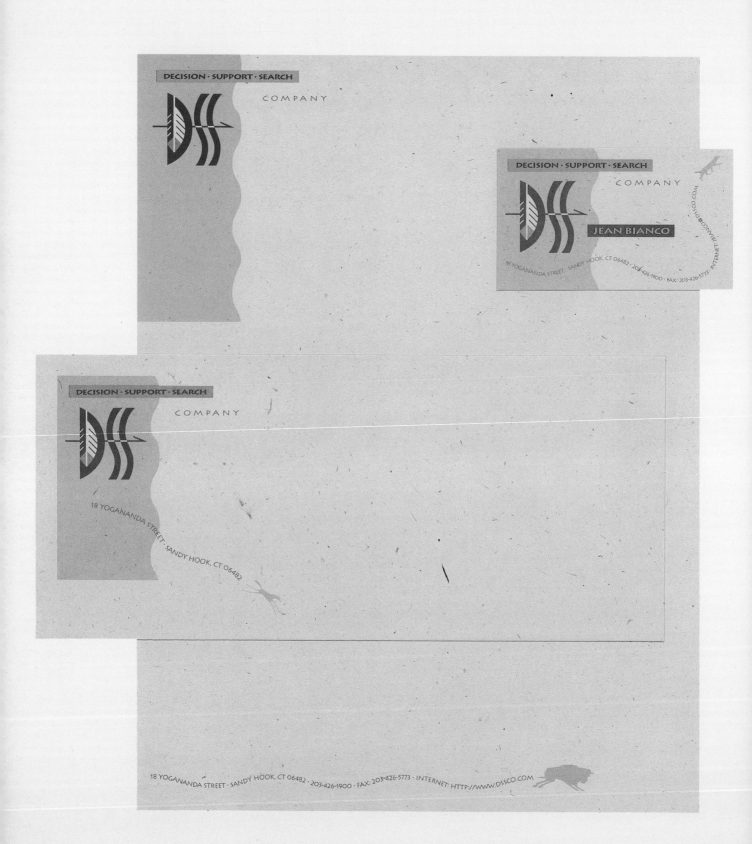

creative firm: **CRSR DESIGNS, INC.**
designer: **Constance R. Snyder**
client: **CRSR Designs, Inc.**

There's not much of an edge-matching problem here, but just the idea of cutting out each of these little squares could cause a hand cramp.

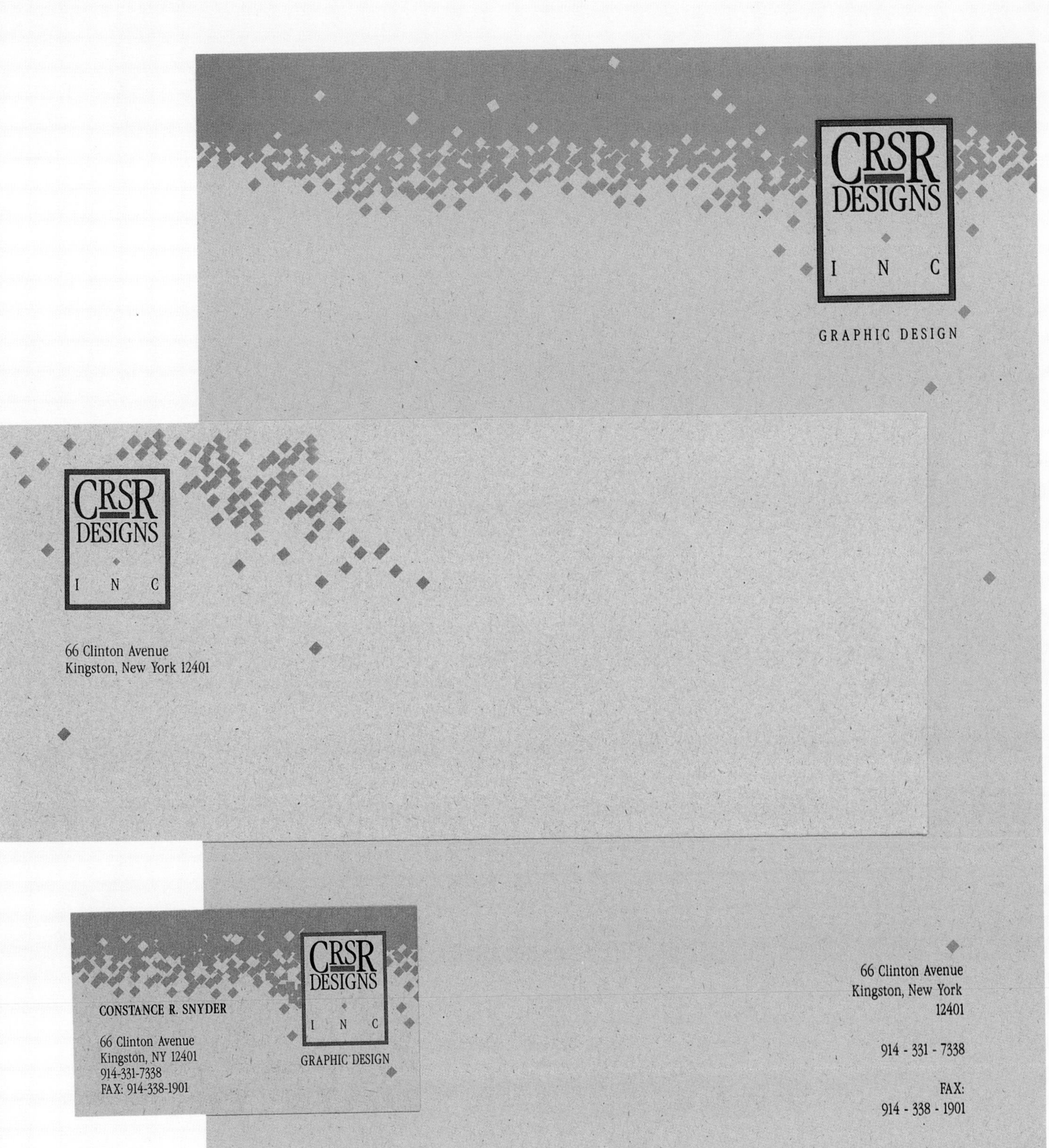

creative firm: SAYLES GRAPHIC DESIGN
designer: John Sayles
client: 1998 Iowa State Fair

This fantastic use of color would have required four layers of amberlith. Yes, all those circles would have had to have been cut. Yes, those fine-lined ovals would have had to have been cut. Yes, those seemingly random-edged backgrounds would have had to have matched exactly...

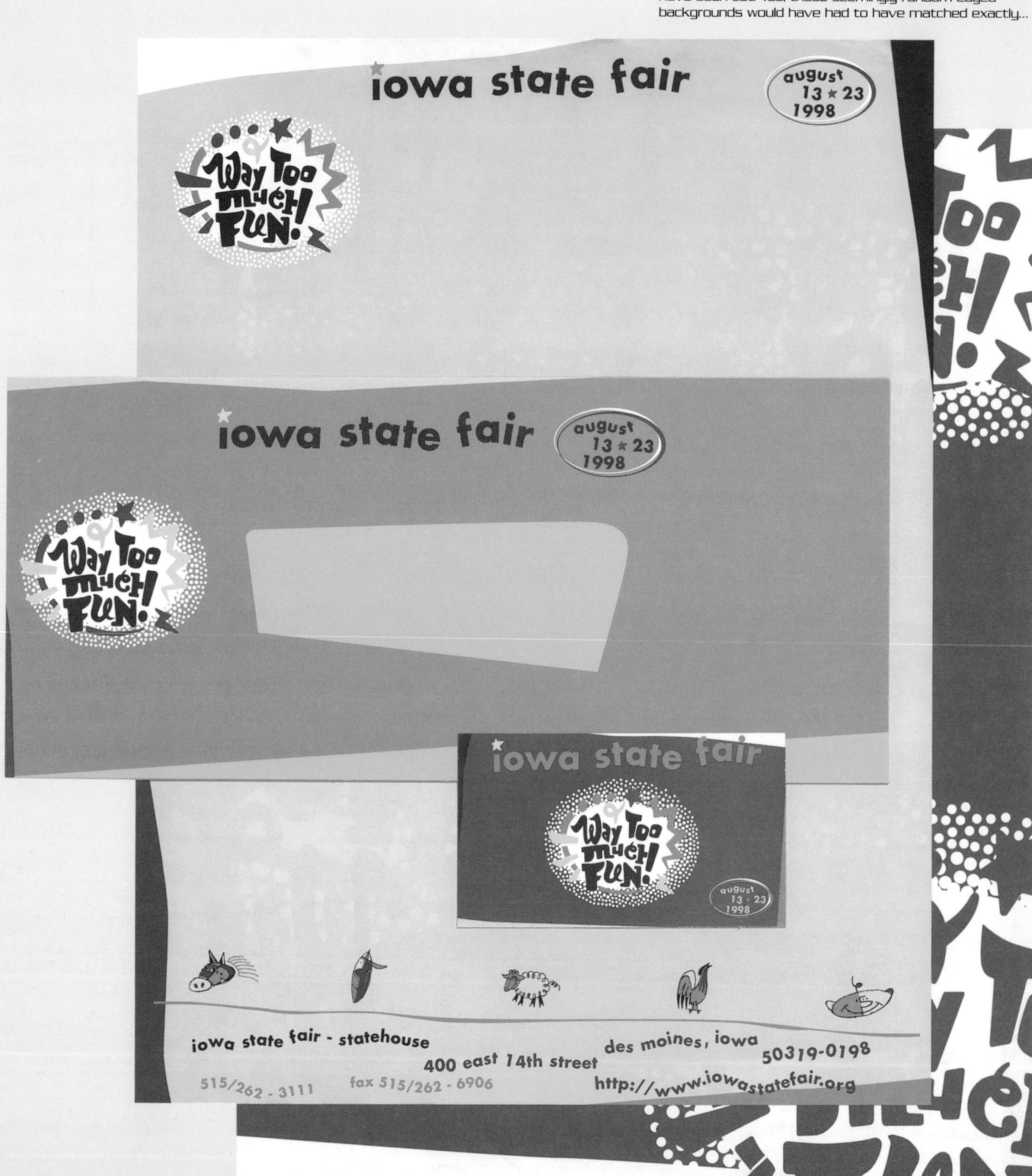

creative firm: CADMUS/O'KEEFE
designer: Brian Thomson
client: Azalea Films

It only looks like one magenta ink on the business card, but three percentages equals three different overlays (just of the magenta)!

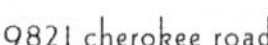

richmond, virginia 23235

tel : 804 . 323 . 5740

fax : 804 . 320 . 5461

9821 cherokee road
richmond, virginia 23235

Fonts and font manipulation exploded with computer-generated design and the aid of Postscript. Being able to roughen, scale, crop, color, fade, reflect, blur, skew, and mix types opened graphic options that had been left largely unexplored. Fonts are now relatively inexpensive and the designer has thousands from which to choose.

Text manipulation has also improved. Gone are the days of sending copy to be set at a type house (where you picked from the fonts they had on hand). Now, perfect tabs, leading, kerning, tracking, multiple sizes, and paragraph options offer the opportunity for all of us to learn to become skilled typesetters.

creative firm: **GLYPHIX STUDIO**
designers: Brad Wilder, Brad Brizendine
client: Diamondsoft

Lots of fonts are readily accessible for use in a single document.

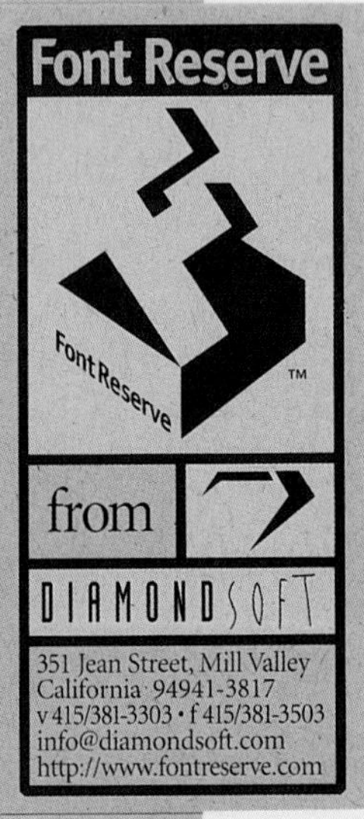

creative firm: **YUGUCHI & KROGSTAD, INC**
designer: **Cifford Yuguchi, Stuart Araki**
client: **SurLuster Inc.**

Flipped type with an applied gradient is a snap with computer-capabilities.

SurLuster Inc.
11601 Wilshire Blvd.
Suite 2410
Los Angeles
CA 90025
Phone: 310 914-3086
800 871-5600
Fax: 310 914-3087

SurLuster Inc.
11601 Wilshire Blvd.
Suite 2410
Los Angeles
CA 90025

SurLuster Inc.
11601 Wilshire Blvd.
Suite 2410
Los Angeles
CA 90025
Phone: 310 914-3086
Fax: 310 914-3087
E-mail: takamakz@ibm.net

Kazunari Takama
President

creative firm: **FORD & EARL ASSOCIATES, INC.**
designer: **Todd Malhoit**
client: **Jerome Duncan, Inc.**

The tab function of many programs can offer perfect alignment or stacking every time.

JEROME DUNCAN

JEROME • DUNCAN INC.
8000 FORD COUNTRY LANE
STERLING HEIGHTS, MI 48313

GREG MUSHRO

JEROME DUNCAN

JEROME • DUNCAN INC
VAN DYKE @ 17 1/2 MILE
STERLING HEIGHTS, MI 48313
DIRECT, 24 HR ACCESS 810 977 6309
FAX 810 826 8487
INTERNET www.jeromeduncan.com
EMAIL greg@jeromeduncan.com

JEROME • DUNCAN INC.
VAN DYKE @ 17 1/2 MILE
STERLING HEIGHTS, MI 48313
DIRECT: 810-268-7500
FAX: 810-826-8487
INTERNET: www.jeromeduncan.com
E-MAIL: ford@jeromeduncan.com

creative firm: CUBE ADVERTISING & DESIGN
designer: David Chiow
client: dreyfus + associates Photography

Effects can make type much more visually interesting.

2101 locust street st. louis, missouri 63103

dreyfus + associates PHOTOGRAPHY

t 314 436 1988
f 314 436 7943

dreyfus@stlnet.com

2101 locust street st. louis, missouri 63103

dreyfus + associates PHOTOGRAPHY

t 314 436 1988
f 314 436 7943

dreyfus@stlnet.com

creative firm: A E R I A L
client: A E R I A L

A design firm with logos strong in typography mixes them almost Minimalistly with visuals and other fonts.

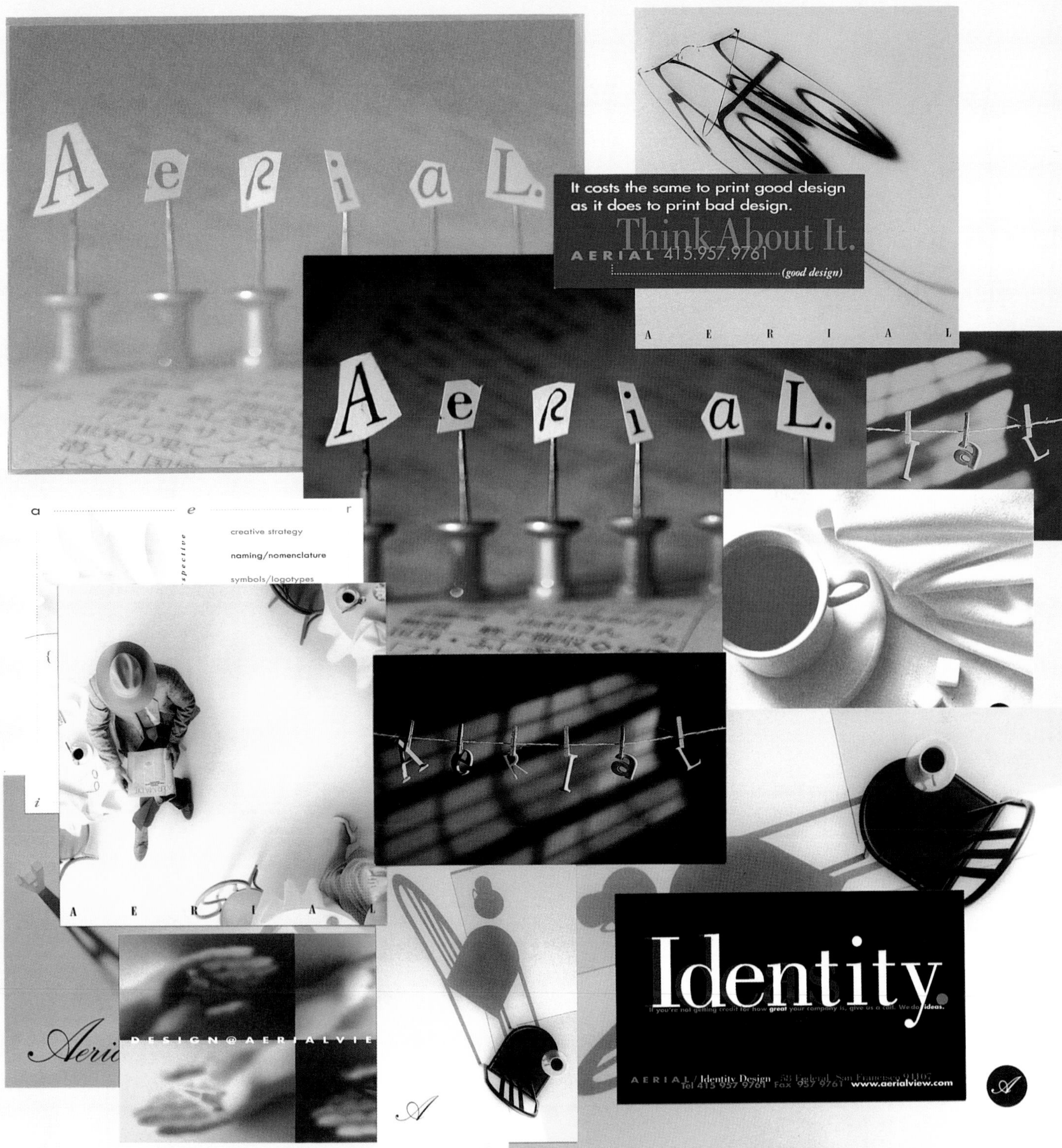
AeRiaL
It costs the same to print good design
as it does to print bad design.
Think About It.
AERIAL 415.957.9761
(good design)
A E R I A L
AeRiaL
a e r
creative strategy
naming/nomenclature
symbols/logotypes
A E R I A L
DESIGN@AERIALVIE
Identity.
AERIAL / Identity Design
Tel 415 957 9761 Fax 957 9761 www.aerialview.com

creative firm: **SARGENT & BERMAN**
designer: **Pete Sargent**
client: **Pep Products, Inc.**

Type doesn't just communicate through reading. Special treatments also make strong informational statements.

Pep Products, Inc.
3130 N. Commerce Ct.
Castle Rock, CO 80104-8002

Tammi Rozar
National Brand Manager

Pep Products, Inc.
8018 East Santa Ana Canyon Rd.
Suite 100-157
Anaheim, California 92808
Tel: 714.998.1179
Fax: 714.998.5760
Corporate Headquarters: 800.624.4260

Pep Products, Inc.
3130 N. Commerce Ct.
Castle Rock, CO 80104
Tel: 800.624.4260
Fax: 303.688.1591

creative firm: THIBAULT PAOLINI DESIGN ASSOCIATES
designer: Judy Paolini
client: Bix Pix Entertainment

A bit of technological irony: the vast array of computerized fonts offers calligraphic and typewriter typefaces for an un-computerized look.

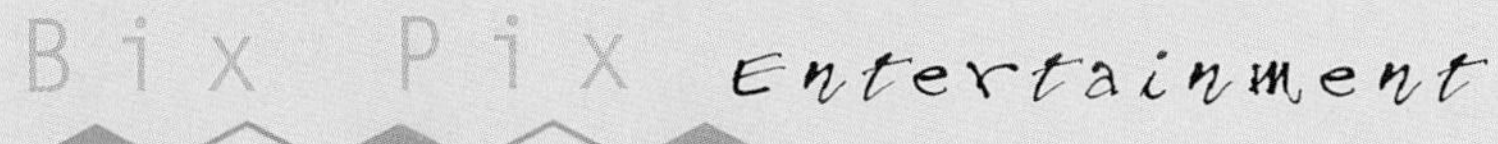

creative firm: **BOLING ASSOCIATES**
designer: **Jeff Barkema**
client: **Boling Associates**

Using different font styles and sizes in accordance with each other can create a dynamic design.

BOLING ASSOCIATES
Advertising·Marketing
Communications

BOLING ASSOCIATES
Advertising·Marketing
Communications

Advertising

BOLING ASSOCIATES

BOLING ASSOCIATES
Advertising·Marketing
Communications

BOLING ASSOCIATES
5100 N. Sixth Street,
Suite 120 Fresno, CA 93710
BRAD BOLING
President
T 209 244.4922
F 209 244.5740

5100 N. Sixth Street,
Suite 120 Fresno, CA 93710
T 209 244.4922 F 209 244.5740

creative firm: MILLENNIUM DESIGN
designer: Michele LaPointe
client: The Lemmings

Mixing a freely-rendered type and a more traditional one accentuates both.

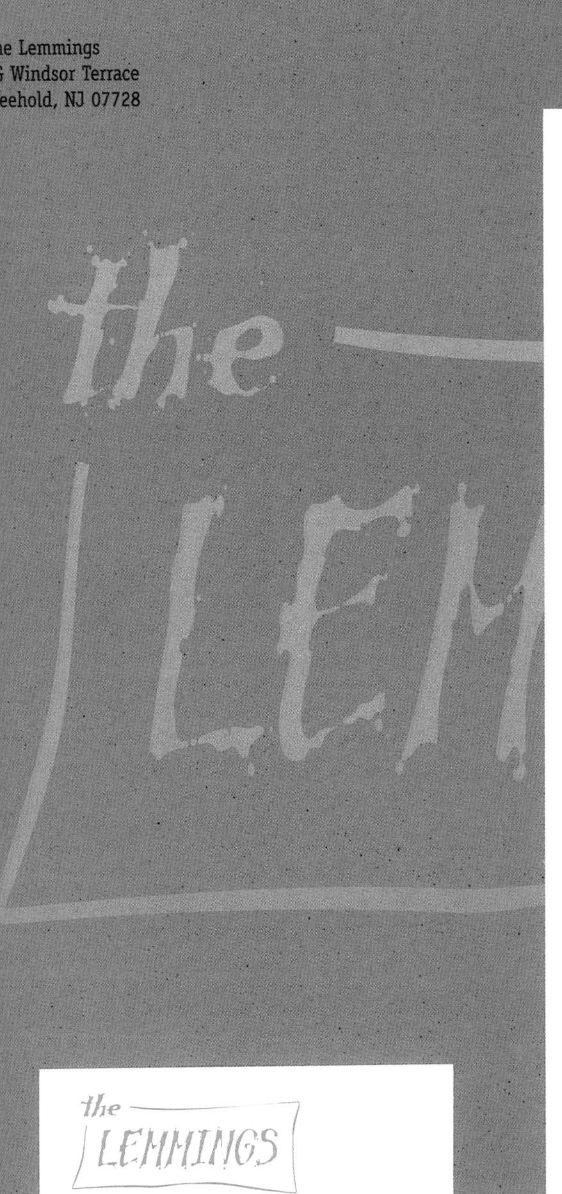

creative firm: **ROBERT MOTT & ASSOCIATES**
designers: **Robert Mott, Kathy Wise**
client: **Namale Resort**

Letters can actually be drawn and scanned, or fonts can be created, but a plethora of the freer grunge typefaces makes it easy to project a nice uncomputerized look.

creative firm: WORDS OF A FEATHER
designer: Melissa Titone
client: Words of a Feather

A hand-lettered work can be scanned for consistent use in computer files.

Creating a gradient fill for an object involves at least two colors changing from one to the other. A gradient from black to white would employ several percentages of gray between the two "end" colors. Depth and dimension often result from gradients. A blend, on the other hand, may well include gradient colors, but also integrates two separate objects. A red square transformed into a green circle is a blend. These techniques would have been nearly impossible before the use of Macintosh.

creative firm: GENSLER
designers: Patricia Glover, Cathrine Noe
client: The Parkside Group

A circle turns into an orb with a radial gradient fill.

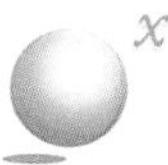

THE PARKSIDE GROUP
Strategic Equity Investors

Barry L. Schneider
Managing Partner

THE PARKSIDE GROUP
Strategic Equity Investors

THE PARKSIDE GROUP
Strategic Equity Investors

Barry L. Schneider
Managing Partner

650 California Street
Suite 2400
San Francisco
California 94108

telephone 415. 393.0630
facsimile 415. 393.0636
e-mail BLSatTPG@aol.com

a limited liability corporation

650 California Street Suite 2400 San Francisco California 94108 *telephone* 415. 393.0630 *facsimile* 415. 393.0636 *e-mail* BLSatTPG@aol.com
a limited liability corporation

creative firm: **TEAMDESIGN**
designer: **Tan Le**
client: **Aditi**

The lattice imagery on this stationery is much more effective with a gradient filling each "slat".

ADITI

ADITI

10940 NE 33rd Place, Suite 204
Bellevue, WA 98004-1432

creative firm: **SARGENT & BERMAN**
designer: Peter Sargent
client: Toolbox Productions, Inc.

Streaming light is represented by subtle gradients dissolving into a lighter shade of pale.

The three-dimensionality of the toolbox might be the result of carefully placed gradients, but is more likely highlight and shadow shapes blended into the basic form.

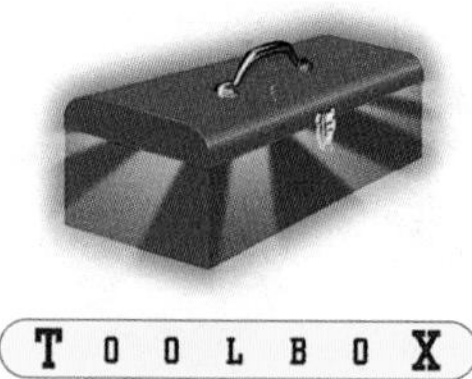

TOOLBOX

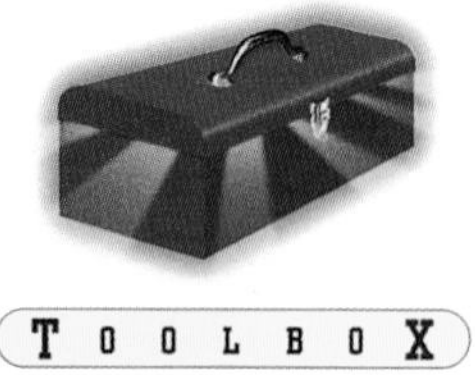

TOOLBOX

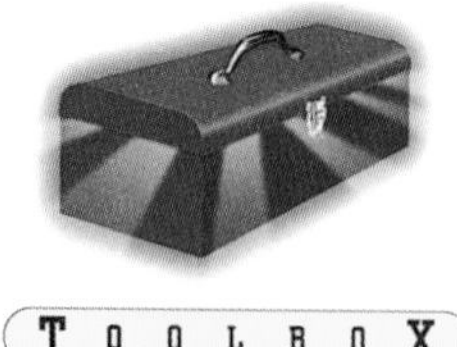

TOOLBOX

Toolbox Productions, Inc.
11800 Wilshire Blvd.
Los Angeles, California 90025
Tel 310.575.7180
Fax 310.575.7227
e-mail PROMOBOX @aol.com

Toolbox Productions, Inc.
11800 Wilshire Blvd.
Los Angeles, California 90025
Tel 310.575.7180
Fax 310.575.7227
e-mail PROMOBOX @aol.com

creative firm: **PUSH**
designers: **Steve Barretto, Todd Foreman**
client: **Revolution**

This swirl couldn't have been effected with a simple gradient. However, a blend of different colored arcs turns into a vortex.

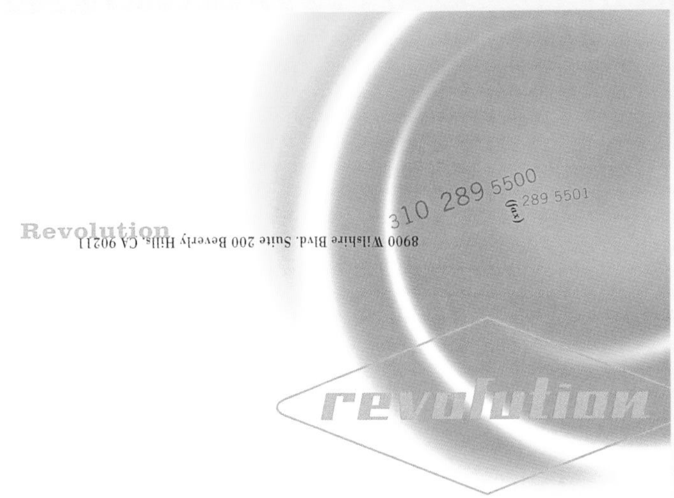

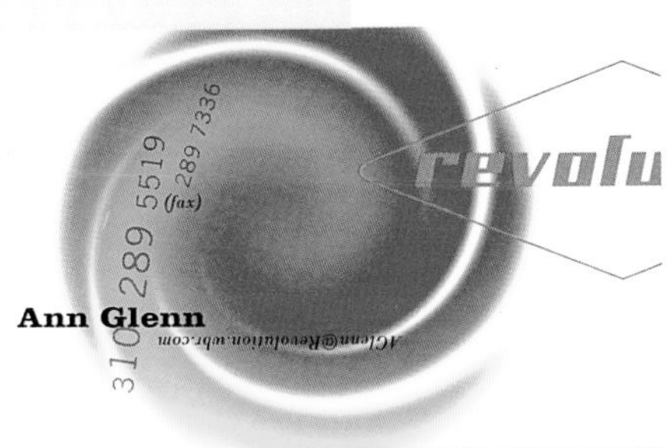

creative firm: **PINK COYOTE DESIGN, INC.**
designer: **Joel Ponzan**
client: **Elance, Corp.**

The globe-like bullet becomes the focus of this logo with a radial gradient filling the circle, and black-to-white fills guiding the viewer's eye to the center.

élancé

Elancé Corp.
Advanced Computing Solutions
730 Fifth Avenue, 9th Floor
New York, New York 10019
Telephone: **212-333-8712**
E-mail: **elance@msn.com**
Fax: **212-333-8720**

Linda Hunter
President & CEO

Elancé Corp.

A subsidiary of Hunter Rozsell Information Services, Inc.

730 Fifth Avenue, 9th Floor

New York, New York 10019

Elancé Corp.

A subsidiary of Hunter Rozsell Information Services, Inc.

730 Fifth Avenue, 9th Floor, New York, New York 10019

Telephone: 212-333-8712 • Fax: 212-333-8720

creative firm: HILLIS MACKEY
designer: John Hillis
client: Hillis Mackey

A simple gradient in the background can add to the visual interest of a logo.

1550 Utica Avenue S., Suite 745 · Minneapolis, MN 55416

phone: 612.542.9122 · fax: 612.542.8158

1550 Utica Avenue S., Suite 745 · Minneapolis, MN 55416 · www.hillismackey.com

1550 Utica Avenue South, Suite 745 · Minneapolis, MN 55416 · phone: 612.542.9122 · fax: 612.542.8158 · www.hillismackey.com

creative firm: **DESIGN MOVES, LTD.**
designers: **Laurie Medeiros Freed, Amy Forbes Bunting**
client: **Virtual Media, Inc.**

Gradients can add an effect of vitality. Reversing images (light to dark, and dark to light) avoids repetitiousness while still showing a relationship.

VIRTUAL MEDIA, INC.

18-3 Dundee Road, Suite 300

Barrington, IL

60010-5278

ENGINEERING NEW WORLDS FOR YOU AND YOUR BUSINESS

18-3 Dundee Road

Suite 300

Barrington, IL

60010-5278

Voice: 847.842.9008

FAX: 847.842.1731

www.virtual-media.com

creative firm: BRODKIN & ASSOCIATES, INC.
designer: Carole Brodkin
client: Bayside Technology Group, Inc.

Alternating plum/aqua gradients balance the top and bottom of this logo with a radial center of aqua and white.

BAYSIDE

TECHNOLOGY
GROUP, INC.

BAYSIDE

TECHNOLOGY
GROUP, INC.

47 QUAKER NECK RD.
SALEM, NJ 08079

BAYSIDE

TECHNOLOGY
GROUP, INC.

JOHN A. CIANFRANI
Information Systems Consultant

47 QUAKER NECK ROAD
SALEM, NJ 08079
609-935-5500
FAX 609-935-1288

INFORMATION SYSTEMS CONSULTING
47 QUAKER NECK ROAD, SALEM, NJ 08079 TELEPHONE 609-935-5500 FACSIMILE 609-935-1288

creative firm: **SOLUTIONS BY DESIGN**
designer: **Scott Wong**
client: **Cram**

Angled gradients represent height and distance among geometric images.

DR. ROBERT H.

ORTHODONTIST

DR. ROBERT H.

ORTHODONTIST

DR. ROBERT H.

ORTHODONTIST

Suite 1, Waskasoo Professional Centre
4405 52nd Avenue
Red Deer, Alberta T4N 6S4
Telephone 403.340.8000
Fax 403.342.0201

Lottie Faux, RDA II
New Patient & Treatment Co-ordinator

Robert H. Cram
B.S.c.,D.M.D.,MCl.D.,M.R.C.D.(C)
Certified Specialist In Orthodontics

Suite 1, Waskasoo Professional Centre
4405 52nd Avenue
Red Deer, Alberta T4N 6S4
Telephone 403.340.8000
Fax 403.342.0201

creative firm: TEAMDESIGN, INC.
designer: Karla Chin
client: The Fishin' Place

Concentric ovals with gradient fills realistically suggest waves.

1200 Market Place Tower
2025 First Avenue
Seattle, WA 98121 USA
ph 206.448.9200
fx 206.448.5057

Market Place Tower
First Avenue
e, WA 98121 USA

The Fishin' Place, Inc., General Partner of The Fishin' Place, L.P.

creative firm: **THE TOWNSEND AGENCY**
designer: **Steve Exum**
client: **DK&A**

The gradients on the inside and outside of the curved images in this stationery make a great amount of difference with respect to shadows and highlights.

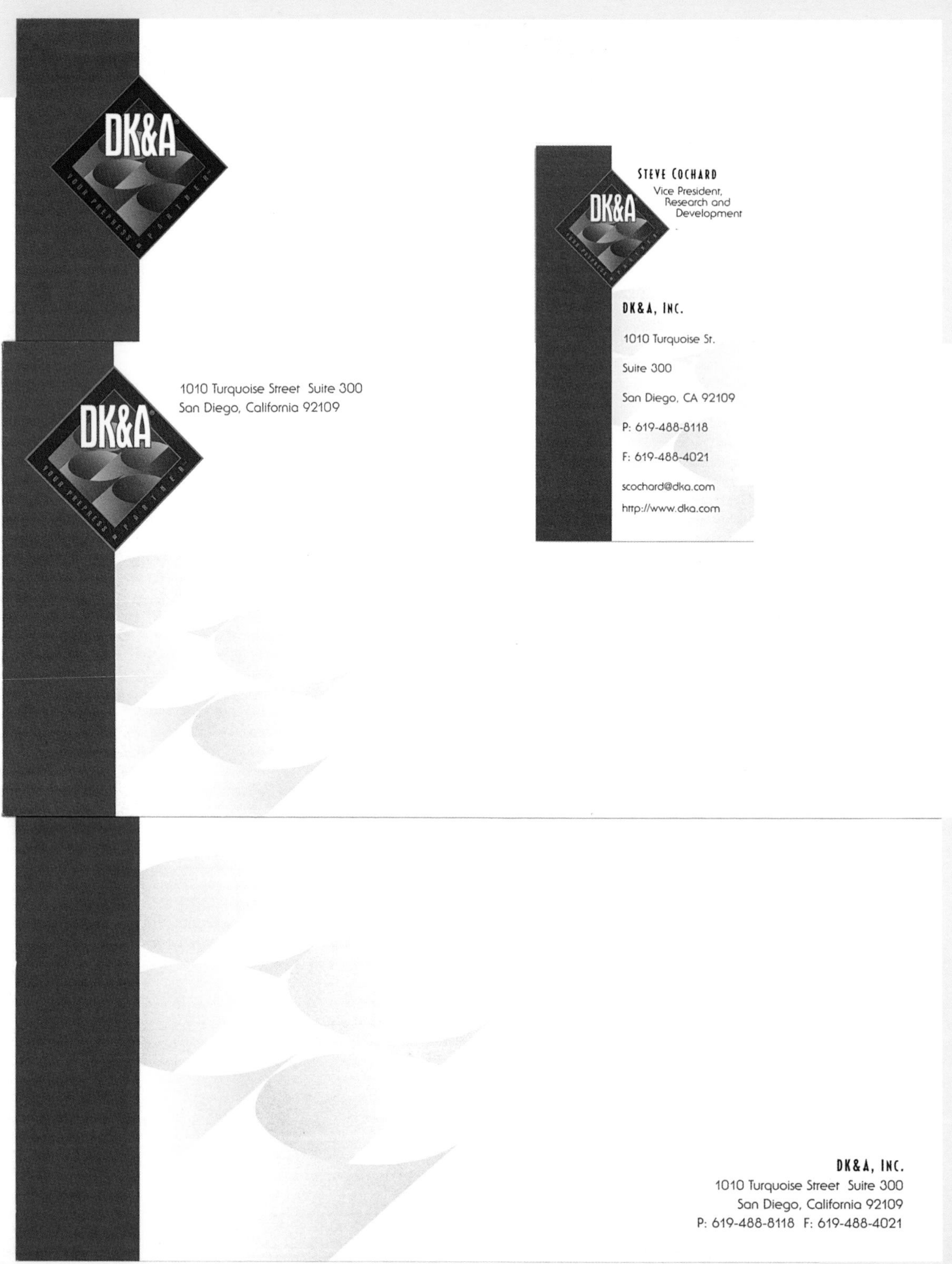

Fantastic detail reproduction can be achieved with digital files. Lines as fine, or finer, than those produced with a technical pen are much easier to draw—and not just straight lines. Original artwork can be scanned and used as a template, or adjusted (in any number of ways) to perfection. Rendering a finely-detailed illustration in its positive form, clicking to change color, and placing it on a dark background so it will print negatively, is much simpler than trying to draw it in negative space.

creative firm: WINTER GROUP
designers: Jennifer Zullo, Wendy Brown
client: Lower Downtown District, Inc.

It might be cost-effective to scan a very detailed image for use. It certainly takes less time to scan than to draw.

Old. New. Now.
LO
DO
DENVER
Christian Brixey
Executive Director
Lower Downtown District, Inc.
1616 Seventeenth Street, Suite 368
Denver, Colorado 80202
303.628.5424 303.628.5495 fax
info@lodo.org www.lodo.org

Old. New. Now.

creative firm: **PAPRIKA COMMUNICATIONS**
designers: **Louis Gagnon, Francis Turgeon**
client: **Paprika**

It would be possible to draw these illustrations by hand, but consistency of line weight is much easier to control with the aid of a computer-drawing program.

creative firm: TAB GRAPHICS DESIGN, INC.
client: TAB Graphics Design, Inc.

A starched, lacy doily is the epitome of detail.

TAB GRAPHICS DESIGN

7550 W. YALE AVE., SUITE A240, DENVER CO 80227
303-985-5999 • FAX 303-985-1023

TAB GRAPHICS DESIGN

7550 W. YALE AVE., SUITE A240
DENVER CO 80227

creative firm: **HORNALL ANDERSON DESIGN WORKS, INC.**
designers: **Jack Anderson, Debra Hampton, David Bates, Lisa Cerveny**
client: **Stewart Capital Management**

Increasing and decreasing image size is much less time consuming than shooting stats. In addition, the designer has the option of scaling or maintaining line weight.

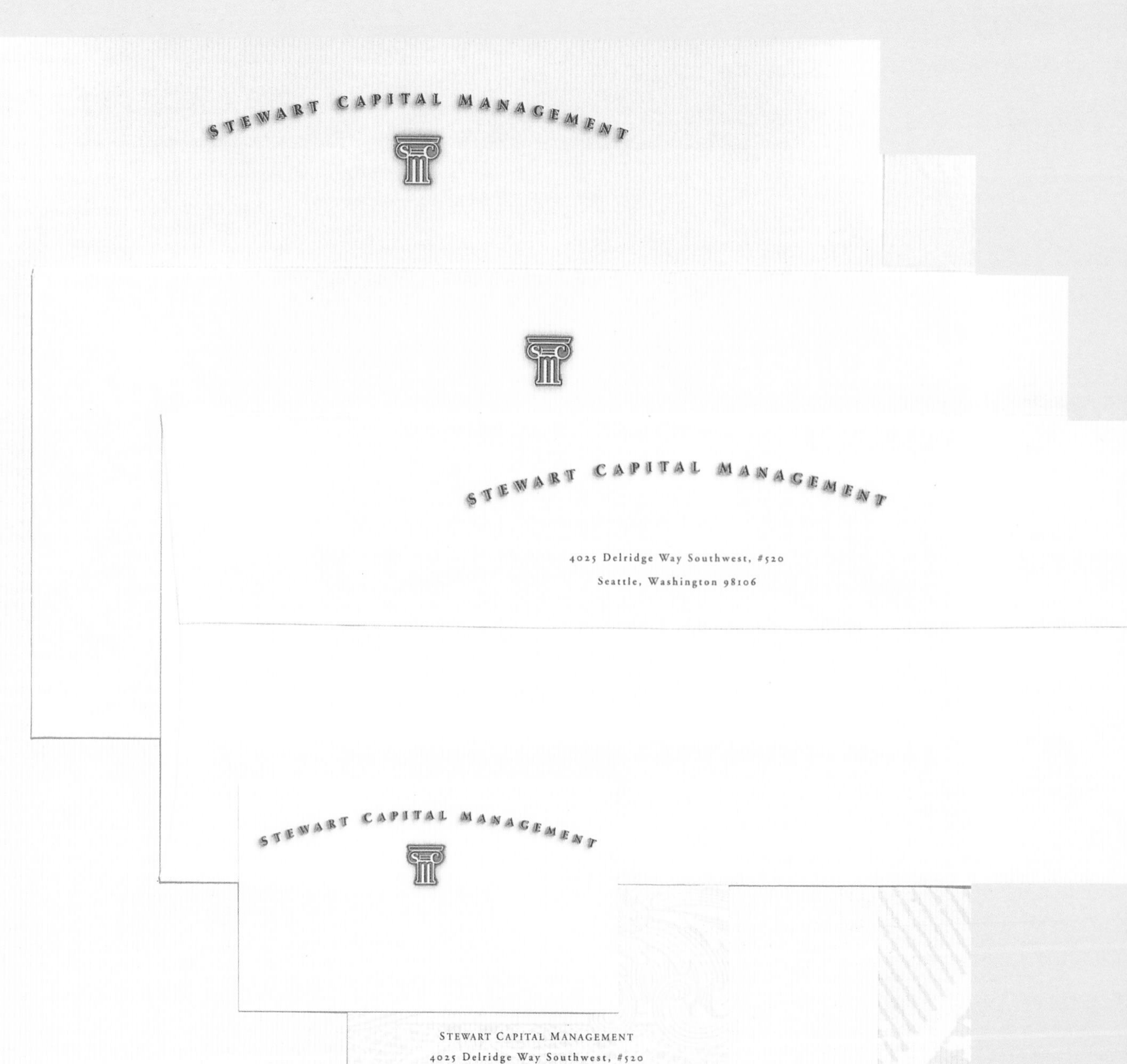

Another door of computer-generated design was opened with the ability to scan photographs or transparencies at high resolution. Now there are even digital cameras which eliminate the need to scan. Without trying to sound like Adobe public relations, the truth is Adobe Photoshop® has been the biggest boon to photographic manipulation since the darkroom. Many other programs, i.e. Specular Collage®, Kai's Photo Soap®...are also useful. Color changes, filter effects, lighting adjustments, and touch ups are a minimal list of what can now be done "at home" with pictures.

creative firm: **PARHAM SANTANA, INC.**
designer: **Rick Tesoro**
client: **Project for Public Space, Inc.**

Different photographs (and the same photograph) treated with different intensities and colors makes an interesting mini mural.

Lila Wallace Reader's Digest
URBAN PARKS
INSTITUTE

Project for
Public Spaces, Inc.
153 Waverly Place
New York, NY 10014

Fred I. Kent, III

Lila Wallace Reader's Digest
URBAN PARKS
INSTITUTE

Project for Public Spaces, Inc.
153 Waverly Place, New York, NY 10014
Tel 212.620.5660, Fax 212.620.3821
E-mail urbparks@usa.pipeline.com

Project for Public Spaces, Inc., 153 Waverly Place, New York, NY 10014, Tel 212.620.5660, Fax 212.620.3821, E-mail urbparks@usa.pipeline.com

creative firm: **THE HOPKINS GROUP**
designers: **Ed Donald, Lynette Bohn**
client: **Gorman's**

Photographic textures are widely available to use alone or incorporate with others.

GORMAN'S
BUSINESS ENVIRONMENT SOLUTIONS

24463 West 10 Mile Road, Southfield, Michigan 48034
(810) 357-6620
FAX (810) 357-0632

creative firm: VOLAN DESIGN LLC
designers: Michelle Van Sauten, Michele Braverman
client: SAP

Monochromatic colors can be applied to specific areas of photos.

5 Westbrook Corporate Center
Westchester, Illinois 60154

creative firm: ENGLE + MURPHY
designers: Emily Moe, Stella Chong
client: CorEvent

Montages are much simpler to produce on a computer than in the darkroom.

236 east 3rd street, suite 210
long beach, california 90802
t. 562.983.7278 f. 562.983.7274

236 east 3rd street, suite 210
long beach, california 90802

Kevin B. Murphy

236 east 3rd street, suite 210
long beach, california 90802
t. 562.983.7278
f. 562.983.7274

creative firm: A E R I A L
designer: Tracy Moon
client: Impact Unlimited

Transparencies or photos can now be recolored and cropped into atypical shapes. all within a digital file

Events

Marketing

Exhibits

Interiors

On Site Services

i! impact UNLIMITED

Events

Marketing

Exhibits

Interiors

On Site Services

Impact Unlimited
250 Ridge Road
Post Office Box 558
Dayton, New Jersey
Zip 08810.0558
Voice 908.274.2000
Fax 908.274.2417

creative firm: **A E R I A L**
designer: **Tracy Moon**
client: **RJ Muna Pictures**

Subtlety often makes a strong statement as is the case with these softly blurred photos, printed in one ink.

creative firm: **KIMBERLY BAER DESIGN ASSOC.**
designer: **Jennifer Miller**
client: **Hauser, Inc.**

Product- or service-specific pictures make an effective setting when utilized as background images.

Hauser Inc
Industrial Design &
Product Development

880 Hampshire Road
Westlake Village
California 91361

phone 805 497 5810
fax 805 497 5820

HAUSER

Mark Capper
Design Research Manage

HAUSER

Hauser Inc
Industrial Design &
Product Development

880 Hampshire Road
Westlake Village CA 9136

phone 805 497 5810
fax 805 497 5820

HAUSER

designer: Michael Lancashire
client: Damian Conrad Photography

Working digitally with photographs can make for a successful marriage between design and photography.

d a m i a n c o n r a d

Damian Conrad Photography

4247 SW Corbett Avenue

Portland, Oregon 97201

P: 503.224.4761

F: 503.224.3452

E: damianc@hevanet.com

W: www.illuminatus.com/dcp

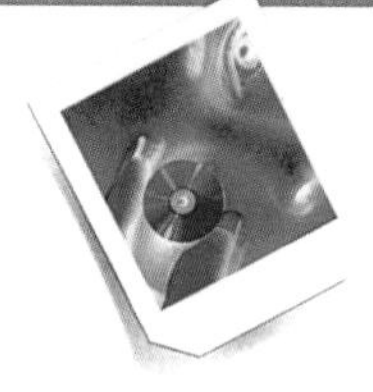

Damian Conrad Photography

4247 SW Corbett Avenue

Portland, Oregon 97201

P: 503.224.4761

F: 503.224.3452

E: damianc@hevanet.com

W: www.illuminatus.com/dcp

d a m i a n c o n r a d

Damian Conrad Photography

4247 SW Corbett Avenue

Portland, Oregon 97201

creative firm: CLARKE & ASSOCIATES
designer: James T. DeVito
client: Clarke & Associates

Whether dealing with symbolism or just pleasing aesthetics, photographs can do it with realism.

c l a r k e & a s s o c i a t e s

V i s i o n

I m a g i n a t i o n

C o m m u n i c a t i o n

c l a r k e & a s s o c i a t e s

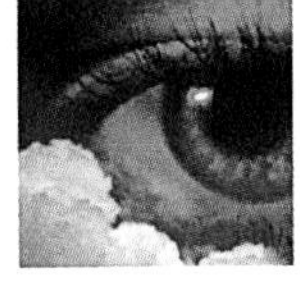

V i s i o n
I m a g i n a t i o n
C o m m u n i c a t i o n

JAMES T. DEVITO
group art director

Vision
Imagination
Communication

c l a r k e & a s s o c i a t e s

40 West High Street
Somerville, New Jersey 08876
908 722 0900 Fax 908 722 0934
e-mail jim@clarke40.com
http://www.clarke40.com

40 West High Street
Somerville, New Jersey 08876
908-722-0900
Fax 908-722-0934
http://www.clarke40.com

creative firm: **GREG WELSH DESIGN**
designer: **Greg Welsh**
client: **LG Interiors**

A fabric photo is a perfect background for an interior designer.

creative firm: PHOENIX CREATIVE, ST. LOUIS
designer: Reid Thompson
client: Gregg Goldman

Beautiful photographs are the major element in this stationery design for a photographer.

gregg goldman
photography
5200 Shaw
St. Louis, MO 63110
tel. 314.771.7227
fax. 314.771.7447
greggphoto@aol.com

creative firm: **WEAVER DESIGN**
designer: **Marie Weaver**
client: **Hunter Films + Photography**

The camera's eye/eye of the photographer is necessarily represented by a photo.

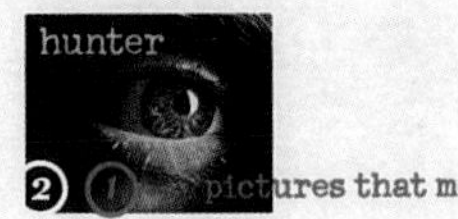

1911 27th Avenue South
Birmingham, AL 35209

pictures that move

pictures
that
move

Hugh Hunter
1911 27th Avenue South
Birmingham, AL 35209
voice (205)879-3153
fax (205)871-0871
email: huntfoto@bham.mindspring.com

hunterphotography

hunterphotography
1911 27th Avenue South
Birmingham, AL 35209
voice (205) 879-3153
fax (205) 871-0871
email: huntfoto@bham.mindspring.com

creative firm: THE PRIME TIME GROUP
designer: John Seymour
client: Roy Anderson Corp

It is very difficult to faux a believable marble texture. With the ready availability of so many varieties of it on disk.

ROY ANDERSON CORP
CONTRACTORS

P.O. Box 2 · Gulfport, Mississippi 39502

ROY ANDERSON CORP
CONTRACTORS

P.O. Box 2 · Gulfport, Mississippi 39502
601·896·4000 · FAX 601·896·4078

creative firm: **SYNERGY DESIGN GROUP**
designers: John LoCastro, David McGowan
client: The Seminole Tribe of Florida Dept. of Archaeology & Genealogy

Though this organization has a nice logo, the photograph printed on the letterhead speaks plainly and directly to its genealogical aspect.

SEMINOLE
anthropology & genealogy

Department of Anthropology & Genealogy
Seminole Tribe of Florida ▾ 6300 Stirling Road ▾ Room 421 ▾ Hollywood, FL 33024 ▾ 954.966.6300 *phone* ▾ 954.967.3423 *fax*

TOMMY JUMPER AND GRANDSON, EDWIN, 1967.

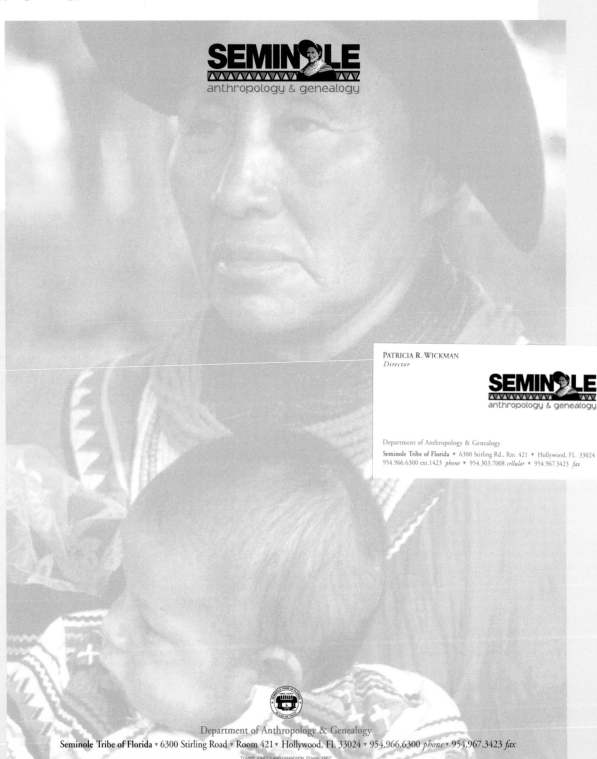

PATRICIA R. WICKMAN
Director

SEMINOLE
anthropology & genealogy

Department of Anthropology & Genealogy
Seminole Tribe of Florida ▾ 6300 Stirling Rd., Rm. 421 ▾ Hollywood, FL 33024
954.966.6300 ext.1423 *phone* ▾ 954.303.7008 *cellular* ▾ 954.967.3423 *fax*

creative firm: **A-HILL DESIGN**
designer: **Sandy Hill**
client: **Robert Reck Photography**

These monochromatic and very artistic shots are wonderful focal points for this photographer's stationery.

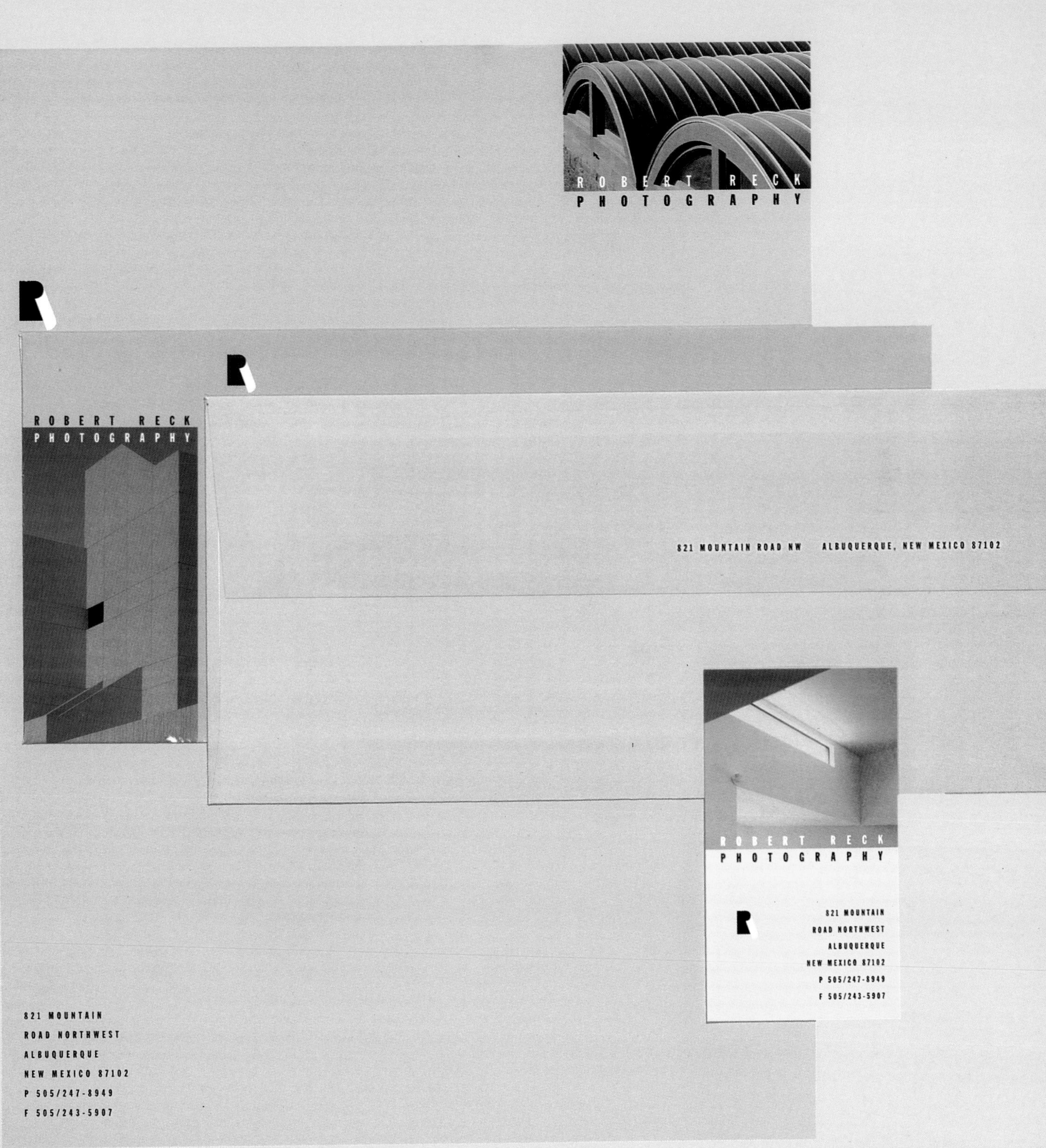

creative firm: **THOMAS RYAN DESIGN**
designer: **Thomas Ryan**
client: **Hart Freeland Roberts**

A vignette portrait of a founding father leaves an impression of stability and familiarity.

HFR ARCHITECTURE

Hart Freeland Roberts, Inc. 7101 Executive Center Drive, Suite 300 Post Office Box 1974 Brentwood, Tennessee 37024-1974 615.370.8500 615.370.8530 Fax email@hfrdesign.com

Protocol Writing
25% Cotton

F. Eugene Freeland, engineer and founding partner of HFR

W. J. Tenison, Jr., Architect
Senior Vice President
Hart Freeland Roberts, Inc.
P. O. Box 1974
7101 Executive Center Drive, Suite 300
Brentwood, Tennessee 37024-1974
615.370.8500 615.370.8530 Fax
email:jtenison@hfrdesign.com

HFR ARCHITECTURE

HFR DESIGN

HFR ENGINEERING

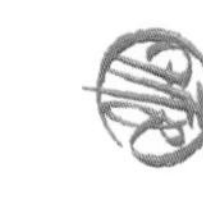

creative firm: **PHOENIX CREATIVE, ST. LOUIS**
designer: **Deborah Finkelstein**
client: **Kelty**

Snapshots can be taken and imported, but sometimes they can be "created". Starting with an original or stock photographic background and adding textures, filter effects or other images, a completely new print is developed.

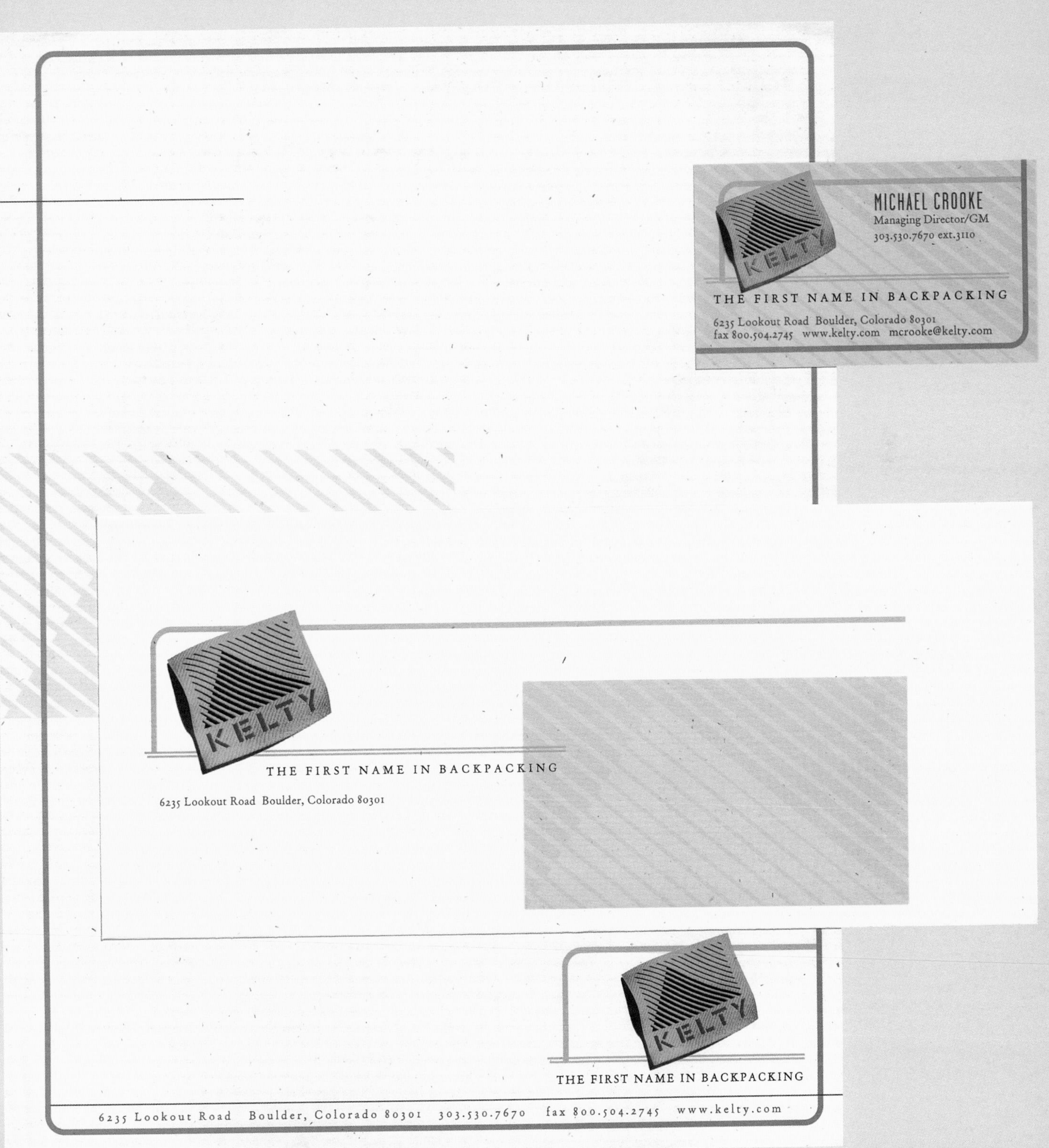

creative firm: **OAKLEY DESIGN STUDIOS**
designer: **Tim Oakley**
client: **Oakley Design Studios**

Portraits, especially of children, always seem to personalize a company's image.

oakley design studios
519 sw park avenue • suite 521
portland, oregon • nine seven two zero five

send to:

tim oakley
creative
oakley design studios
519 sw park avenue
suite 521
portland, oregon
nine seven two zero five
tele: 503-241-3705
fax: 503-241-3812
pager: 503-940-3263
e-mail: oakleyds@teleport.com

oakley design studios
519 sw park avenue • suite 521 • portland, oregon • nine seven two zero five
tele: 503-241-3705 • fax: 503-241-3812 • pager: 503-940-3263 • e-mail: oakleyds@teleport.com

creative firm: **MAYER & MYERS**
designers: **Nancy Mayer, Greg Simmons**
client: **Jamie Rothstein**

Silhouetting, cropping, and applying color can all be achieved with photo manipulation programs.

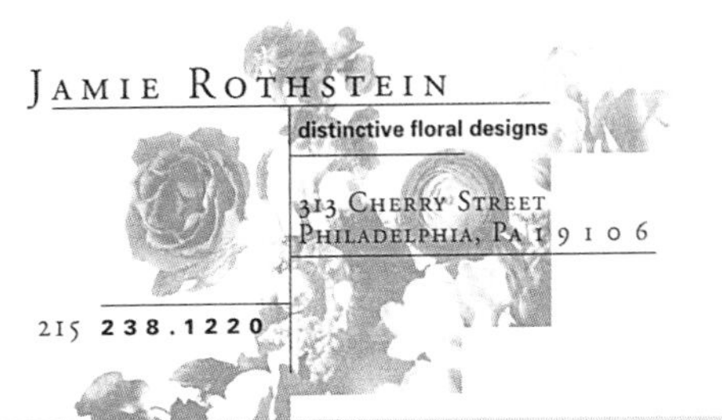

creative firm: **FREYSS DESIGN**
designer: **Christina Freyss**
client: **Freyss Design**

Individual vignettes with consistent characteristics might be used to develop a related theme in design. A single image, distorted and saved as different files, can be utilized in the same manner.

FREYSS DESIGN
205 EAST 22 STREET SUITE 4G NEW YORK NY 10010
TEL·212·683·7708 FAX·212·683·5024

FREYSS DESIGN

creative firm: RAINBOW DESIGN SERVICES
designers: Kim Poulos, Diane Dobler, Peter Aguanno, Caroline Bock
client: The Independent Film Channel

Indistinct and overlapping pictures suggest movement, a good way to represent the film industry through a static medium.

Phone:516.396.3000 Fax:516.364.7638 http://www.ifctv.com

THE INDEPENDENT FILM CHANNEL

150 Crossways Park West, Woodbury, NY 11797

THE INDEPENDENT FILM CHANNEL

150 Crossways Park West, Woodbury, NY 11797

ADVISORY BOARD MEMBERS

Martin Scorsese

Robert Altman

Ethan Coen

Joel Coen

Martha Coolidge

Jodie Foster

Jim Jarmusch

Spike Lee

Tim Robbins

Ed Saxon

Steven Soderbergh

creative firm: **SWANBECK DESIGNS**
designer: **Joshua Swanbeck**
client: **Westgate Family Physicians**

Singular archival images make a simple, but effective design statement for this physicians' office.

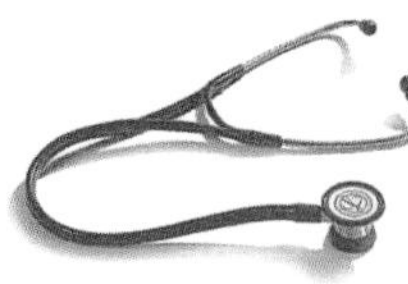

WESTGATE FAMILY PHYSICIANS

GENE M. LEVITZ, MD • BARRY SLATER, MD • JOCELIZA GONZAGA CHAUDHARY, MD

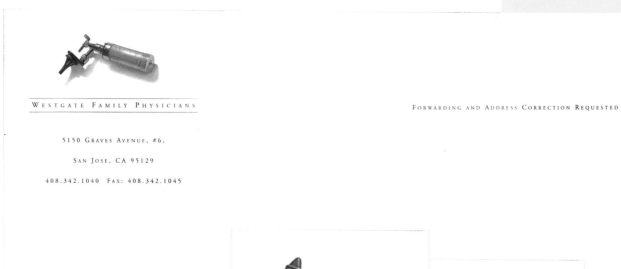

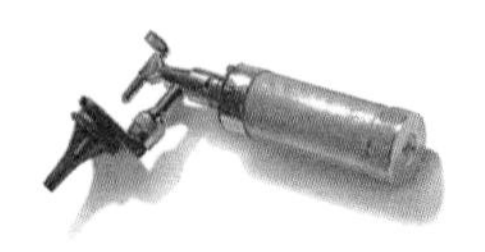

WESTGATE FAMILY PHYSICIANS

5150 GRAVES AVENUE, #6,

SAN JOSE, CA 95129

408.342.1040 FAX: 408.342.1045

FORWARDING AND ADDRESS CORRECTION REQUESTED

WESTGATE FAMILY PHYSICIANS

APPOINTMENT

FOR: __________

DATE: __________

________ AT ________ O'CLOCK

5150 GRAVES AVENUE, #6, SAN JOSE, CA 95129 PHONE: 408.342.1040 FAX: 408.342.1045

Do not think illustrators and computer artists are mutually exclusive. Some purists work with only traditional mediums, but computer illustration offers an opportunity to develop styles more difficult to execute by hand. Never forget the miracle of scanning in accordance with mediums other than Macintosh; sketch it, scan it, use it as a template. Some designers scan an original, using it as is to save costs at the printer. However, drawing and painting programs have become, and continue to become, more advanced with each version offering more control, technical ease, filters, and effects which all lend themselves to the simplicity of creating original artwork by computer.

creative firm: **WELSH + ASSOCIATES**
designer: **Suzann Beck**
client: **Chez Françoise**

It's nice to discover a font that is so perfectly appropriate to an illustration that it looks like part of it.

chez Françoise

chez Françoise

chez Françoise, Inc. • 1023 Main Street • Hopkins, MN 55343

chez Françoise

Chez Françoise, Inc.

1023 Main Street • Hopkins, MN 55343 • (612) 936-0834

chez Françoise, Inc. • 1023 Main Street • Hopkins, MN 55343 • (612) 936-0834

creative firm: **SAYLES GRAPHIC DESIGN**
designer: **John Sayles**
client: **Hotel Fort Des Moines**

Artwork indigenous to Computerland includes bold graphics that call for straight lines.

creative firm: R. BIRD & COMPANY
designers: Richard Bird, Joe Favata
client: R. Bird & Company

Cropping an illustration to repeat a shape or an area is simply executed.

R.BIRD & COMPANY

R.BIRD
& COMPANY

R.BIRD
& COMPANY

Design for Marketing
and Information

R.Bird & Company Inc
150 East 52nd Street
New York NY 10022 USA

Kevin Lenahan
Design Associate

212 317 8307
klenahan@rbird.com

Design for Marketing
and Information

R.Bird & Company Inc
150 East 52nd Street
New York NY 10022 USA
212 317 8300
http://www.rbird.com

Design for Marketing and Information | R.Bird & Company Inc · 150 East 52nd Street · New York NY 10022 USA · 212 317 8300

creative firm: **WEBSTER DESIGN ASSOCIATES**
designers: **Dave Webster, Sean Heisler**
client: **Gold Circle Entertainment**

Though most of these lines are freely-rendered, note the consistent weight of each.

creative firm: **GROUP C DESIGN**
designer: Jenny Azubike
client: Silver Screen

Spot color is a snap (or would that be click?) to apply.

SILVER SCREEN, INC.

(314) 727.0077

Pershing Avenue Saint Loui

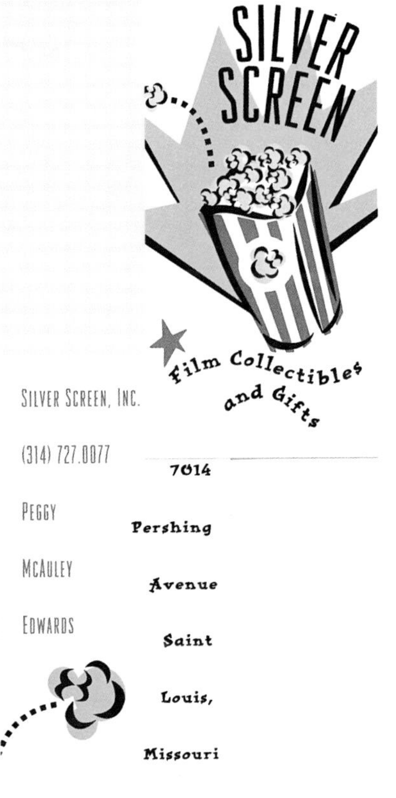

SILVER
SCREEN

Film Collectibles
and Gifts

7014 Pershing Avenue Saint Louis, Missouri 63130

creative firm: **MIRIELLO GRAFICO, INC.**
designers: **Courtney Mayer, Ron Miriello**
client: **Divan**

Filters that offer a blur effect can really soften an illustration—kind of like airbrushing or smudging, but no dirty hands.

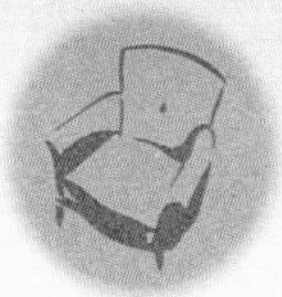

D I V A N

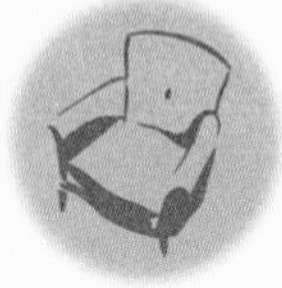

D I V A N

7661 GIRARD AVE.
LA JOLLA, CALIFORNIA
9 2 0 3 7

D I V A N

7661 GIRARD AVE. LA JOLLA, CALIFORNIA 92037
PH 619.551.0405 FAX 619.551.0639

7661 GIRARD AVE. LA JOLLA, CALIFORNIA 92037 PH 619.551.0405 FAX 619.551.0639

creative firm: JCNB DESIGN
designer: Jane Nass Barnidge
client: Stonehouse Farm Goods

Creating collages is an efficient process with a mask or background transparency option.

N5373 County W
Princeton, WI 54968

N5373 County W

Princeton, Wisconsin 54968

(414) 295 4755

Fax (414) 295 4756

Deborah Hernandez
Vice President/Sales

N5373 County W
Princeton, WI 54968
(414) 295 4755
Fax (414) 295 4756

creative firm: **ART KIRSCH GRAPHIC DESIGN**
designers: **Art Kirsch, Charlotte Kirsch**
client: **Searsville Land Company**

Incorporating type into an illustration is certainly easier via computer.

3301 El Camino Real, Suite 200
Atherton, California 94027-3844

Thomas E. Lodato
President

3301 El Camino Real, Suite 200, Atherton, California 94027-3844
Telephone 415-365-0673, Telecopier 415-365-1645

3301 El Camino Real, Suite 200, Atherton, California 94027-3844. Telephone 415-365-0673, Telecopier 415-365-1645

creative firm: **RANDAZZO & BLAVINS, INC.**
designer: **Alan Blavins**
client: **Reynard Printing**

Not all artwork used in digital files is created on a computer, but there are some amazing painterly effects out there.

REYNARD
FINE PRINTING
& LITHOGRAPHY
1275 FAIRFAX AVENUE
SAN FRANCISCO, CA 94124
(415) 861-3448
FAX (415) 641-9840

REYNARD
FINE PRINTING
& LITHOGRAPHY
1275 FAIRFAX AVENUE
SAN FRANCISCO, CA 94124
(415) 861-3448

REYNARD
FINE PRINTING & LITHOGRAPHY
1275 FAIRFAX AVENUE
SAN FRANCISCO, CA 94124
(415) 861-3448 FAX (415) 641-9840

KEVIN HICKEY

creative firm: UNICOM
designer: Ken Eichenbaum
client: Marva Collins Preparatory School of Wisconsin

Even illustrative images finding their roots in the graffiti arena, can be reproduced on the computer.

MARVA COLLINS PREPARATORY SCHOOL OF WISCONSIN

2449 North Thirty-Sixth Street
Milwaukee, Wisconsin 53210
Telephone 414 445.8020
Fax 414 445.8167

MARVACOLLINSPREP

Robert Rauh, PRINCIPAL

BOARD OF ADVISORS

Jr. Bridgeman
Dr. LaRoyce Chambers
Marva Collins
Pastor Michael Dudley
Micky Sadoff
Ronald Sadoff
Dr. Earnestine Willis

Micky Sadoff

MARVACOLLINSPREP

MARVA COLLINS PREPARATORY SCHOOL OF WISCONSIN
2449 North Thirty-Sixth Street, Milwaukee, Wisconsin 53210
Telephone 414 445.8020
Fax 414 445.8167

LICENSED BY M.C. SEMINARS, INC.

MARVACOLLINSPREP

2449 North Thirty-Sixth Street
Milwaukee, Wisconsin 53210

LICENSED BY
M.C. SEMINARS, INC.

creative firm: COMCORP, INC.
designer: Dave Lawrence
client: Delphi Energy Fund

A nice repetition of line makes an energetic statement.

566 WEST ADAMS SUITE 700 CHICAGO, ILLINOIS 60661 TEL 312.258.9400 FAX 312.258.9405

566 WEST ADAMS SUITE 700 CHICAGO, ILLINOIS 60661

BRIAN P. LINEHAN
PRESIDENT

566 WEST ADAMS SUITE 700 CHICAGO, ILLINOIS 60661
TEL 312.258.9400 FAX 312.258.9405

creative firm: **ADDISON WHITNEY**
designer: **Lori L. Earnhardt**
client: **e-Tribe electronic media**

This illustration gives the appearance of a simplistic shape, but drawing it by hand, with the precision the company needs in its logo, would be next-to-impossible.

4011 WestChase Blvd.
Suite 120
Raleigh NC
27607

4011 WestChase Blvd.
Suite 120
Raleigh NC 27607
919.856.0094
fx 919.856.0084

http://www.e-tribe.com

4011 WestChase Blvd. Suite 120 Raleigh NC 27607 919.856.0094 fx 919.856.0084

creative firm: CAGNEY + McDOWELL
designer: Caroline McAlpine
client: Market Square 2000

Relating type and an illustrative style in one digital file is a much more straightforward process than trying to do it while both are separate entities.

MARKET SQUARE 2000 *A Public/Private Partnership*

CO-PRESIDENTS

Prudence R. Beidler

Crissy H. Cherry

BOARD OF DIRECTORS

Howard D. Adams

Pamela K. Armour

Stephen M. Bartram

Judith N. Boggess

Mary F. Casselberry

Stewart S. Dixon

Francis C. Farwell

Jonathan Galloway

Susan E. Garrett

Alice Goltra

David Gorter

Jean M. Greene

Mary Lee Helander

Mary Ann B. Hodgkins

Kennetha L. Krehbiel

Juliet K. Priebe

Lawrence C. Ross

EX OFFICIO

Cornelius B. Waud

CITY LIAISON

Daniel Reeves

LANDSCAPE ARCHITECT

Rodney Robinson

MARKET SQUARE 2000

A Public/Private Partnership

Prudence R. Beidler
Co-President

20 South Stonegate
Lake Forest, IL 60045
Phone 847 234 3277
Fax 847 615 1633

MARKET SQUARE 2000

creative firm: **BOELTS BROS. ASSOCIATES**
designers: Eric Boelts, Jackson Boelts, Kerry Stratford, Diana Freshwater
client: The Freshwater Group

Scratchboard effects can be drawn positively, colored, and placed on black.

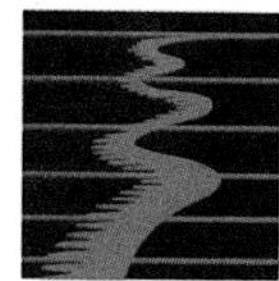

2224 EAST ADAMS STREET
TUCSON, AZ 85719 USA
PH 520.327.7850
FX 520.321.1858
dbf@primenet.com

THE FRESHWATER GROUP

DIANA BARNES FRESHWATER
PRINCIPAL

THE FRESHWATER GROUP

2224 EAST ADAMS STREET
TUCSON, AZ 85719 USA
PH 520.327.7850
FX 520.321.1858
dbf@primenet.com

creative firm: ST. GEORGE GROUP
designer: Kevin Popovic
client: EMi

Drawings with a woodcut look are popular. Comparatively, the computer version is child's play to execute.

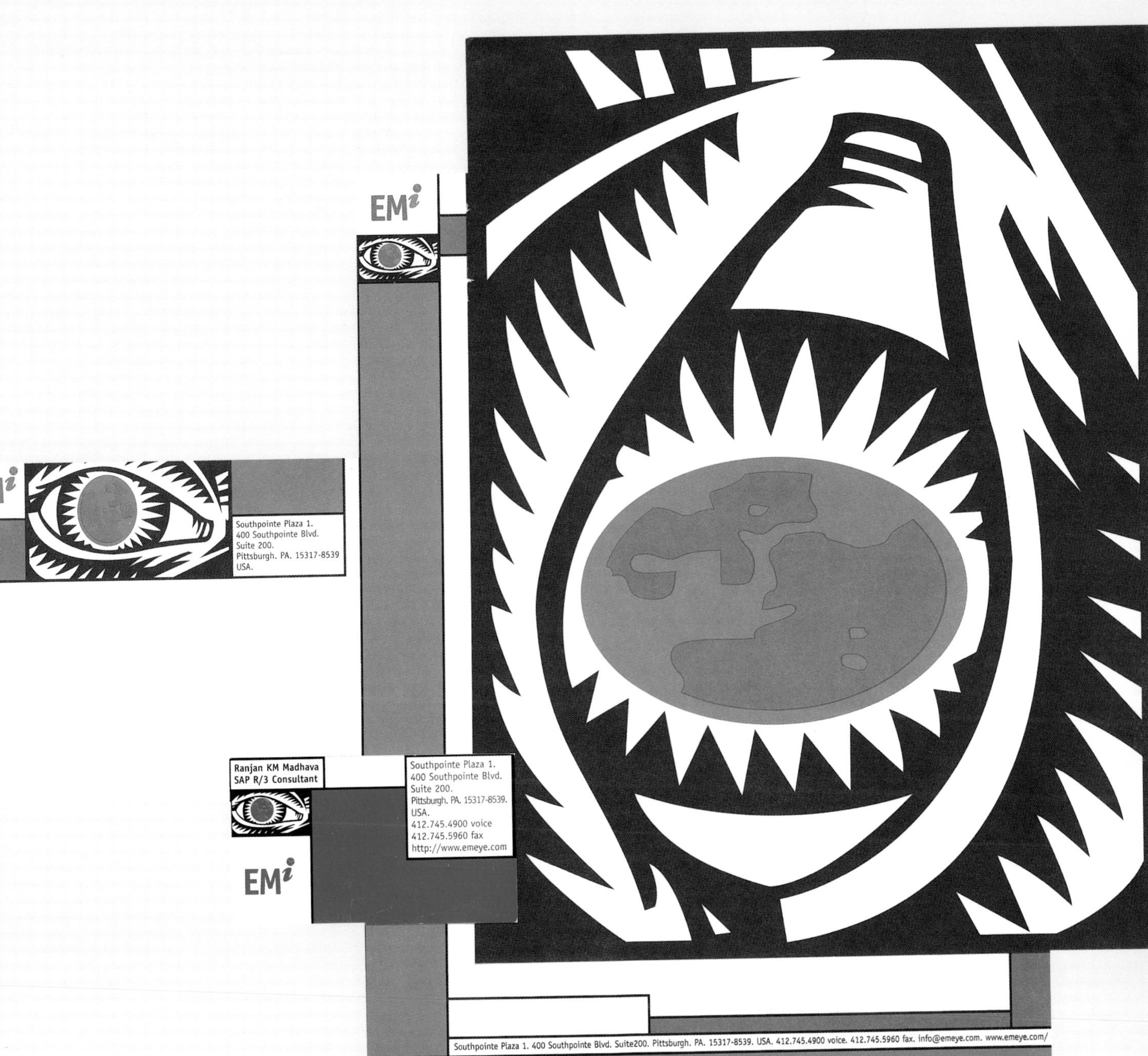

creative firm: **DESIGN ENTERPRISE**
designer: **Scott Crider**
client: **Metropolis Music Recording and Production**

The most efficient way to develop an illustration around a letter from a particular font is in a drawing program.

440 DUBLIN AVENUE
COLUMBUS, OHIO 43215
614 • 224 • 3373

MUSIC AND PRODUCTION FOR
ADVERTISING & INDUSTRY
MUSIC RECORDING FOR
COMMERCIAL RELEASE
AUDIO POST-PRODUCTION
FOR VIDEO

440 DUBLIN AVENUE
COLUMBUS, OHIO 43215
614 • 224 • 3373

creative firm: BULLET COMMUNICATIONS, INC.
designer: Tim Scott
client: Muzyka + Son Funeral Home

All computer drawings don't have to shout. Sometimes a quiet symbol is perfect.

Muzyka & Son
FUNERAL HOME

5776 West Lawrence Ave. • Chicago, Illinois 60630 • Tel: 773/545-3800 • Fax: 773/545-1996

Since 1915

Muzyka & Son
FUNERAL HOME

5776 West Lawrence Ave. • Chicago, Illinois 60630

Since 1915

Muzyka & Son
FUNERAL HOME
Since 1915

David Kulawiak
Director

West Lawrence Ave. • Chicago, Il 60630
el: 773/545-3800 • Fax: 773/545-1996

The ability to create drop and cast shadows used to require a vast amount of technical knowledge, skill, and manipulation. Now it can all be done through the use of a filter and a couple of mouse clicks. (Some stock photography companies include a choice of shadows for each image in eps form.) The simplicity of execution in no way decreases the strength of the shadow's three-dimensional effectiveness.

creative firm: **HORNALL ANDERSON DESIGN WORKS, INC.**
designers: **Jack Anderson, Julie Keenan, Larry Anderson**
client: **Alta Beverage Company**

Some shadow options include an allover shadow which results in a kind of glowing effect.

ALTA

ALTA

ALTA BEVERAGE CORPORATION
10189 MCDONALD PARK ROAD, SUITE 11
SIDNEY, B.C. V8L 5X5

ALTA

ANN L. EVANS
PRESIDENT

(604) 655-3512 FAX (604) 655-3369
ann@altabeverage.com

ALTA BEVERAGE CORPORATION
10189 MCDONALD PARK ROAD, SUITE 11, SIDNEY, B.C. V8L 5X5
PHONE (604) 655-9235 FAX (604) 655-0209
http:\\www.altabeverage.com
e-mail: mail@altabeverage.com

creative firm: **ART KIRSCH GRAPHIC DESIGN**
designer: **Art Kirsch**
client: **Art Kirsch Graphic Design**

Shadows can define depth between design elements.

4160 Byron Street, Suite B, Palo Alto, CA 94306. Phone/Fax: 415-493-5867. E-mail: artkirsch@aol.com

creative firm: **TERRY O COMMUNICATIONS (1993) INC.**
designer: **Terry O'Connor**
client: **S'port for Kids Foundation**

A design element can be treated to stand out a little from the rest with a cast or drop shadow.

9030 Leslie Street
Suite 6
Richmond Hill
Ontario L4B 1G2
Tel: (905) 886-4392
Fax: (905) 886-6617

Terry O'Connor
Director of Promotion

9030 Leslie Street, Suite 6
Richmond Hill, Ontario L4B 1G2
Tel: (905) 886-4392
Fax: (905) 886-6617

STATIONERY HAS BEEN CREATED THROUGH THE GENEROSITY OF SOMERSET GRAPHICS CO. LTD., NORTH CAMBRIDGE KUMON CENTRE AND TERRY O COMMUNICATIONS (1993) INC.

creative firm: SULLIVAN MARKETING & COMMUNICATIONS
designer: Jack Sulllivan
client: Alliance Marketing Solutions

Shadows can lift type off the page.

3104 East Camelback Road • Suite 439 Phoenix, Arizona 85016-4595 • 602.954.8850 • Fax: 602.971.4733

3104 East Camelback Road • Suite 439 Phoenix, Arizona 85016-4595

ALLIANCE:
Marketing Solutions

Bill Watson

ALLIANCE:
Marketing Solutions

3104 East Camelback Road, Suite 439
Phoenix, Arizona 85016-4595
602.954.8850/Direct: 602.224.4701
Fax: 602.423.1821
email: bwatson@cyberpub.com

creative firm: WEBSTER DESIGN ASSOCIATES
designers: Dave Webster, Sean Heisler
client: Gold Circle Entertainment

A cast shadow can add more height and depth to an image's position than a drop shadow can.

Gold Circle
ENTERTAINMENT

Gold Circle
ENTERTAINMENT

Michael Delich
PRESIDENT & CEO

Gold Circle
ENTERTAINMENT

13906 GOLD CIRCLE
SUITE 201
OMAHA, NE 68144
TEL 402.330.2520
FAX 402.330.2445
WWW.GOLDO.COM

13906 GOLD CIRCLE SUITE 201 OMAHA, NE 68144
TEL 402.330.2520 FAX 402.330.2445 WWW.GOLDO.COM

creative firm: COOK SHERMAN
designers: Ken Cook, I-Hua Chen
client: Digital Imaging Group

Several techniques are used to draw attention to the "dig" in digital, including a drop shadow.

creative firm: **SYNERGY DESIGN GROUP**
designers: **John LoCastro, Dave McGowan**
client: **Freedom Fabrication**

The purple logo element seems to hover with the aid of its shadow.

815 North Main Street Suite B ▪ Havana, Florida 32333
800.304.FREE 904.539.4194 904.539.4195 *fax*

815 North Main Street Suite B ▪ Havana, Florida 32333

FREEDOM
FABRICATION

815 North Main Street Suite B
Havana, Florida 32333

800.304.FREE
904.539.4194
904.539.4195 *fax*

Rick Redmond

e-mail freedomfab@oandp.com
web site www.oandp.com/freedomfab

e-mail address
freedomfab@oandp.com

web site
www.oandp.com/freedomfab

Drawing swirls and spirals used to be a rather happenstance event, making many attempts until one of them "looked right". A great improvement was the computer drawing program which offered lines with anchors points that had handles. This allowed the designer/ illustrator to make curves on various planes that would result in a spiral. Now there's a spiral tool with options and adjustments. Could it be easier?

creative firm: **PHINNEY/BISCHOFF DESIGN HOUSE**
designers: **Juli Saeger, Leslie Phinney**
client: **Phamis Incorporated**

Spirals are indicative of movement and orbits.

CORPORATE HEADQUARTERS
1001 Fourth Avenue Plaza, Suite 1500
Seattle, WA 98154-1144

CORPORATE HEADQUARTERS
1001 Fourth Avenue Plaza, Suite 1500 Seattle, WA 98154-1144 T 206•622•9558 FX 206•667•9712
http://www.phamis.com

creative firm: **ZUNDA DESIGN GROUP**
designers: **Charles Zunda, Jon Voss**
client: **Zunda Design Group**

This fantastic swirl wasn't created push-button style. Beginning with a harder-edged original, it was built in Photoshop, imported into Lightwave 3D where it was angled and rendered; brought back into Photoshop and given its final tweaking for a dynamic, soft, textured image.

creative firm: **COOKSHERMAN, INC.**
designers: **Ken Cook, Inka Mulia**
client: **Liquid Audio**

A nice spiral defines the top edge of the letterhead paper.

SCOTT BURNETT
Vice President of Marketing
415.562.0880
sburnett@liquidaudio.com
TM
LIQUID AUDIO
2421 Broadway Second Floor Redwood City CA 94063 FAX 562.0899 www.liquidaudio.com

2421 Broadway Second Floor Redwood City CA 94063 415.562.0880 FAX 562.0899 www.liquidaudio.com

creative firm: **SHELBY DESIGNS & ILLUSTRATES**
designer: **Shelby Putnam Tupper**
client: **The Bock Company**

This double-looped swirl is an integral part of the initial logo.

At one time technical pens, straight edges, and french curves were the only way to get the desired line weight and path. It was not easy. For various reasons, India ink didn't always flow smoothly from the pen tip. The tiniest glob or smudge was enough to ruin an entire piece no matter good the rest of it looked. The most visually successful technique was to produce the desired art in a much enlarged version and reduce it with a stat camera. That way, slight imperfections diminished to imperceptibility. Never, never, never was increasing an original a viable option. The smoothest, tightest line blown up 200% suddenly became a silhouette of the Rocky Mountains.

creative firm: SCHAFER
designer: Brian Priest
client: Schafer

Drawing circles was difficult at best. Even with a circular template, as opposed to creating a circle with a French curve, the pen point had to maintain the same spatial relationship to the template for the entire line, or dips and bumps were evident.

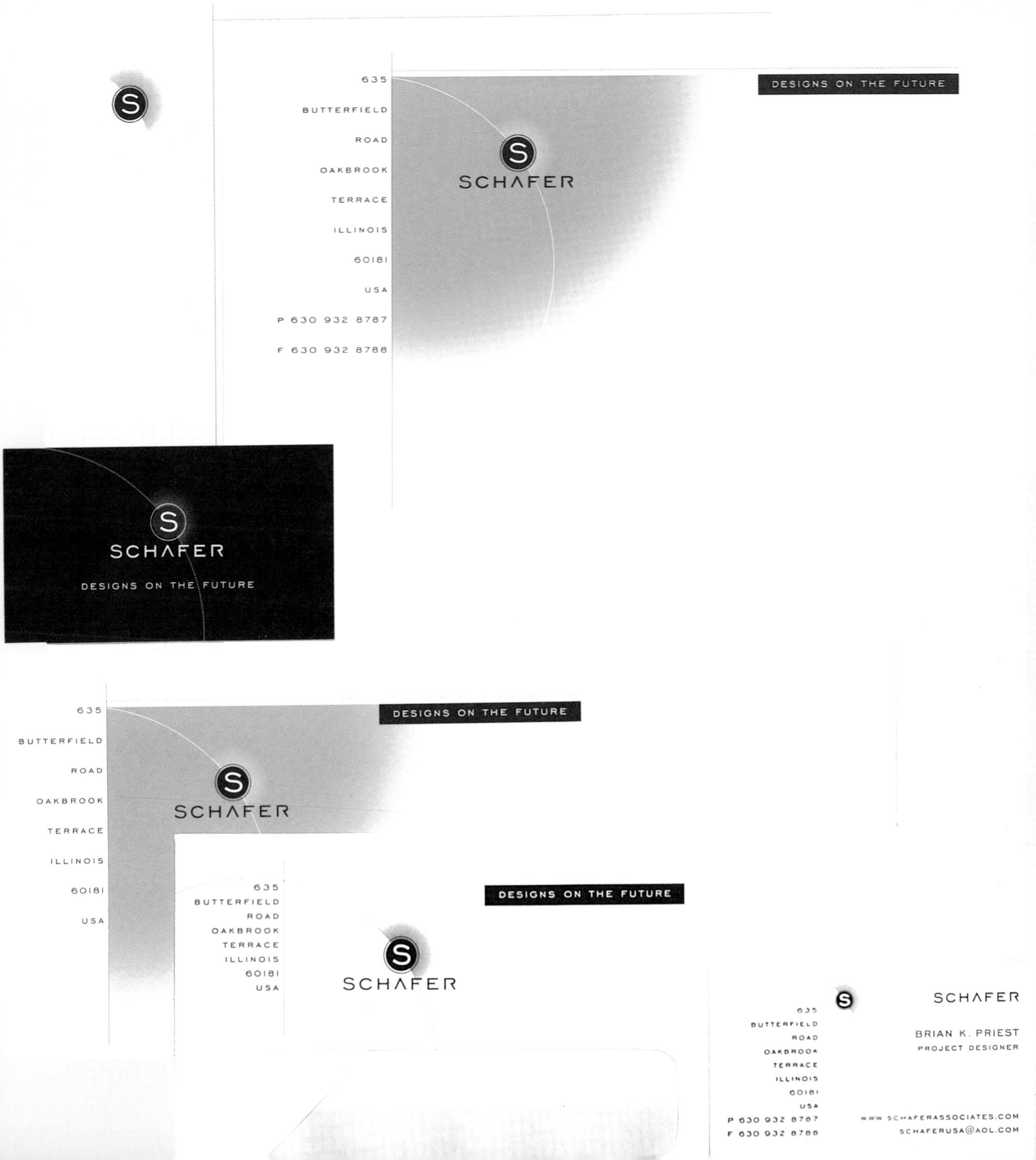

S

635
BUTTERFIELD
ROAD
OAKBROOK
TERRACE
ILLINOIS
60181
USA
P 630 932 8787
F 630 932 8788

DESIGNS ON THE FUTURE

S
SCHAFER

S
SCHAFER
DESIGNS ON THE FUTURE

creative firm: R. BIRD & COMPANY
designers: Joe Favata, Richard Bird
client: Dynalog Technologies Ltd.

A clean-looking arch is simply executed in a drawing program.

DYNALOG TECHNOLOGIES LTD
401 COLUMBUS AVENUE
VALHALLA NY 10595

CORPORATE
COMPUTER
PROFESSIONALS

DOV J. GOLDMAN • PRESIDENT

DYNALOG TECHNOLOGIES LTD
401 COLUMBUS AVENUE
VALHALLA NY 10595

TEL 914-747-4477
FAX 914-747-3930
DGOLDMAN@DYNALOG.COM

DYNALOG TECHNOLOGIES LTD
401 COLUMBUS AVENUE
VALHALLA NY 10595

on a relentless quest
for productivity

TEL 914-747-4477
FAX 914-747-3930
MAIL@DYNALOG.COM

creative firm: **VISUAL MARKETING ASSOCIATES, INC.**
designer: **Lynn Sampson**
client: **Visual Marketing Associates, Inc.**

Hairlines of consistent weight were particularly difficult to render.

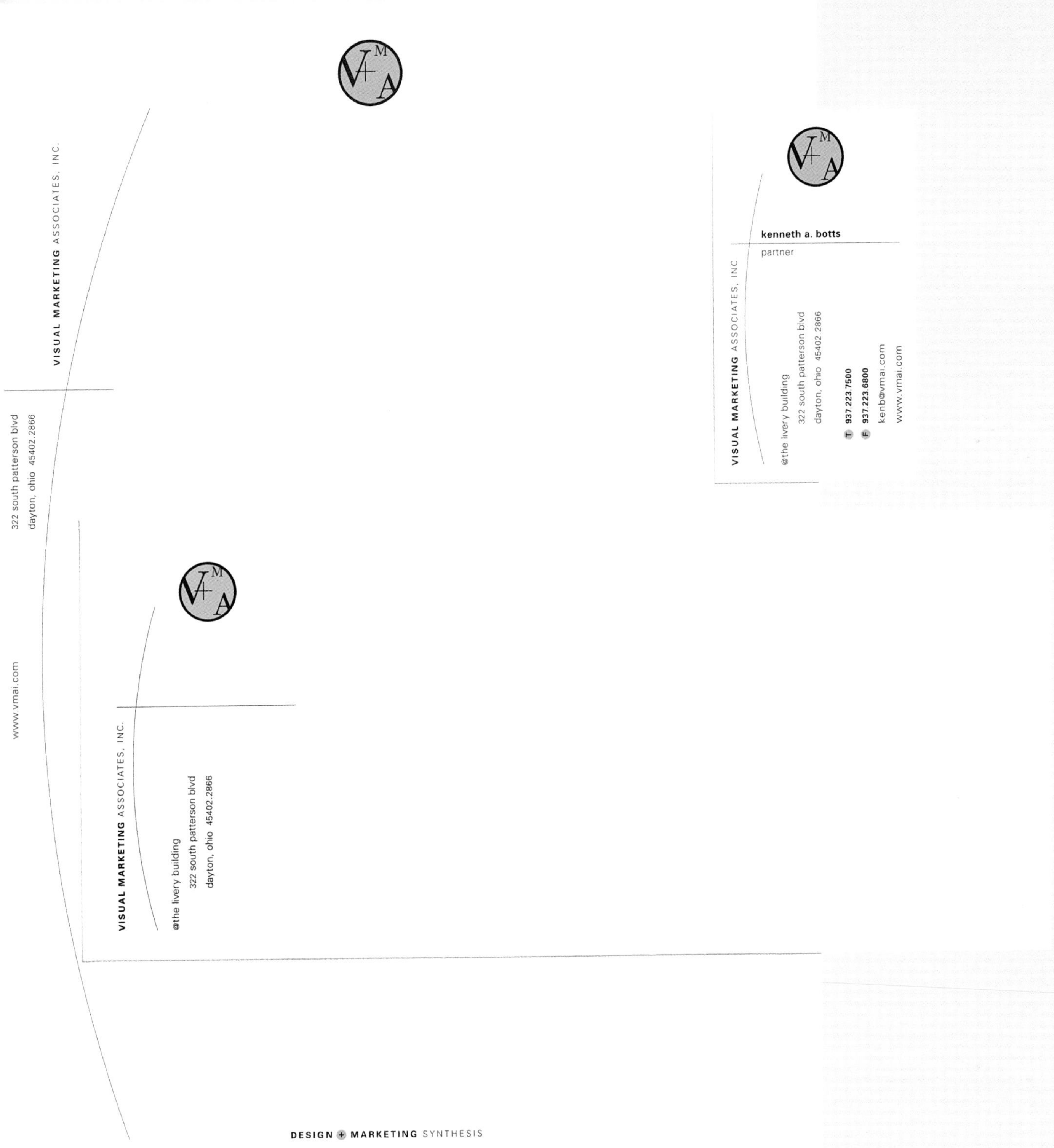

VISUAL MARKETING ASSOCIATES, INC.
322 south patterson blvd
dayton, ohio 45402.2866
www.vmai.com

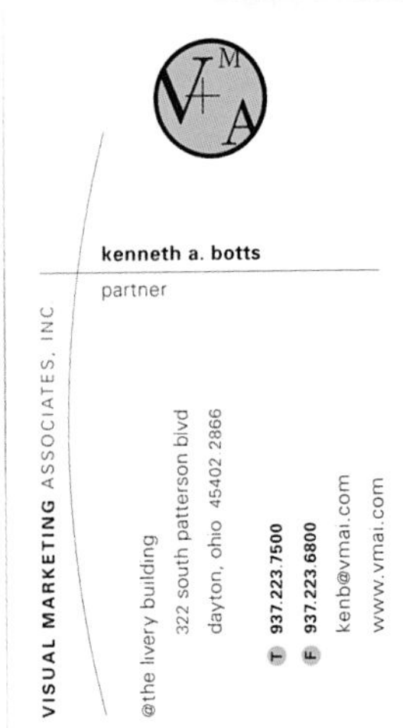

VISUAL MARKETING ASSOCIATES, INC.
@the livery building
322 south patterson blvd
dayton, ohio 45402.2866

DESIGN + MARKETING SYNTHESIS

creative firm: **ROBERT MEYERS COMMUNICATION DESIGN & PLANNING**
designer: **Robert Meyers**
client: **PSO—Pittsburgh Symphony Orchestra**

Symmetrical curves can be made by copying, flipping, and joining.

600 Penn Avenue,
Pittsburgh, PA 15222-3259

412 392 4826 Fax 412 392 3311
600 Penn Avenue, Pittsburgh, PA 15222-3259

creative firm: **SOLUTIONS BY DESIGN**
designer: Liz Roberto
client: Tate

All lines are not solid black. Some are constructed of elements on a path. Placing objects on a path is easier on a computer because the path is easier to draw while the elements can be moved incrementally en masse.

Sigrid E. Tate
DDS • MSD

Orthodontics & Facial Orthopedics
for Children & Adults

Sigrid E. Tate
DDS • MSD

313 South Berkley Road, Suite D
Kokomo, Indiana 46901

Orthodontics & Facial Orthopedics
for Children & Adults

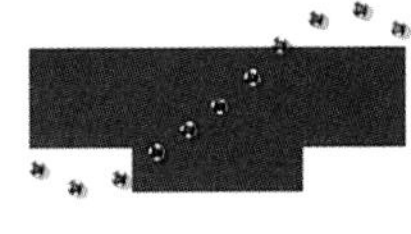

Sigrid E. Tate
DDS • MSD

Orthodontics & Facial Orthopedics
for Children & Adults

313 South Berkley Road
Suite D
Kokomo
Indiana 46901
317/459~3145

313 South Berkley Road, Suite D
Kokomo, Indiana 46901
317/459~3145

creative firm: STREAMLINE DESIGN STUDIO
designer: Kourosh Gorji
client: Streamline Design Studio

Producing perfectly lined spacing between elements is less involved in design by computer.

STREAMLINE DESIGN STUDIO  1875 CALIFORNIA STREET NO.6 SAN FRANCISCO CA 94109

KOUROSH GORJI
Creative Director
STREAMLINE DESIGN STUDIO
1875 California Street NO.6
San Francisco CA 94109
TEL 415 771 8711 FAX 415 771 8716
EMAIL sds@efaxinc.com

STREAMLINE DESIGN STUDIO
1875 CALIFORNIA STREET NO.6 SAN FRANCISCO CA 94109 TEL 415 771 8711 FAX 415 771 8716
E-MAIL sds@efaxinc.com URL www.efaxinc.com/~sds

creative firm: **STUDIO 405**
designers: **MariAnn Donnelly, Jodi Bloom**
client: **The World Bank**

A smooth, hard-edged curve defines space on this letterhead.

1818 H Street, NW
Washington, DC 20433

1818 H Street, NW
Washington, DC 20433

Hotline: 202.473.1222
Phone: 202.458.1450/4508
Fax: 202.522.0500

1818 H Street, NW • Washington, DC 20433
Hotline 202.473.1222 • Phone 202.458.1450/4508 • Fax 202.522.0500

creative firm: **WATERMAN DESIGN**
designer: **Priscilla White Sturges**
client: **The Roussel Collection**

Flowing script "R" from a needle and thread appears as a hands-on creation, but consistent line weight reveals its origin as Macintosh.

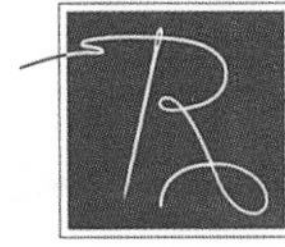

The Roussel Collection

847 Beacon Street
Newton Centre, MA 02159

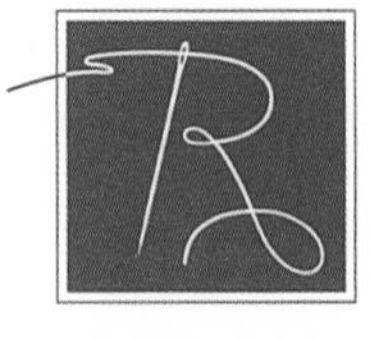

The Roussel Collection

The Roussel Collection

LINDA ROUSSEL

847 Beacon Street, Newton Centre, MA 02159
Telephone 617 964 5657

847 Beacon Street
Newton Centre, MA 02159
617.964.5657

creative firm: GENSLER
designers: Jane Brady, Cathrine Noe, Patricia Glover
client: Giancarlo & Gnazzo

Curved lines can easily maintain straight-edged beginnings and ends with computer design. Handwork involves either cutting a straight edge, or struggling with more technical pen work.

Martin B. Howard
415. 278. 9030

625 Market Street, Suite 1100
San Francisco, CA 94105

tel 415. 541. 0500
fax 415. 541. 0506
martin@gglaw.com

a professional corporation

625 Market Street, Suite 1100, San Francisco, California 94105 telephone 415. 541. 0500 facsimile 415. 541. 0506
a professional corporation

creative firm: **CWA INC.**
designers: **Susan Merritt, Calvin Woo**
client: **MultiSpectra**

Forget all the geometric dynamics of trying to create the logo of concentric circles. Just try to draw that very simple, red, curved line.

6175 NANCY RIDGE DRIVE
SAN DIEGO
CALIFORNIA 92121-3224

619.450.9131
619.450.9179 FAX

CONRAD C. GRELL
VICE PRESIDENT ENGINEERING

6175 NANCY RIDGE DRIVE
SAN DIEGO
CALIFORNIA 92121-3224

619.450.9131
619.450.9179 FAX

cgrell@multispectra.com E MAIL

creative firm: **McKNIGHT/KURLAND DESIGN**
client: **City of Chicago**

Straight edges of a silhouetted version of the logo add visual interest and define space on this letterhead.

1121 S. State, Room 401, Chicago, Illinois 60605

BEYOND THE RHETORIC
Facing the Challenges of
Community Policing

BEYOND THE RHETORIC
Facing the Challenges of
Community Policing

1121 S. State, Room 401, Chicago, Illinois 60605 • Tel 312/747-6208

CITY OF CHICAGO
Richard M. Daley, *Mayor*

creative firm: **LAURIE GOLDMAN DESIGN**
designer: **Laurie Goldman**
client: **Highview Entertainment**

A box bordered with clean, unobtrusive lines highlights text.

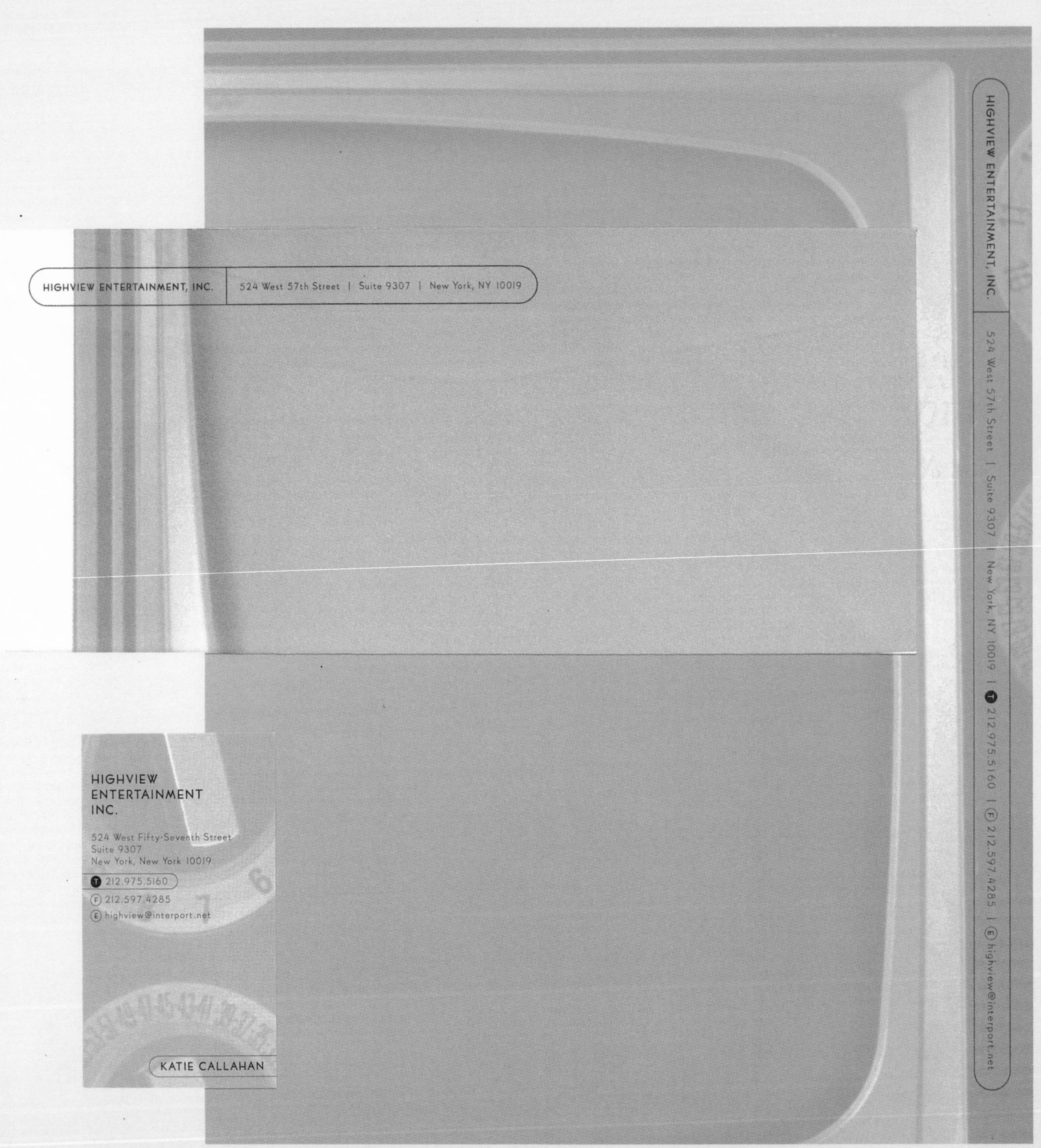

HIGHVIEW ENTERTAINMENT, INC.
524 West 57th Street | Suite 9307 | New York, NY 10019
HIGHVIEW ENTERTAINMENT, INC.
524 West 57th Street | Suite 9307 | New York, NY 10019 | T 212.975.5160 | F 212.597.4285 | E highview@interport.net
HIGHVIEW
ENTERTAINMENT
INC.
524 West Fifty-Seventh Street
Suite 9307
New York, New York 10019
T 212.975.5160
F 212.597.4285
E highview@interport.net
KATIE CALLAHAN

Reducing and enlarging images wasn't really THAT big a deal precomputer. To have camera-ready artwork, all images had to be in position at 100% (or at least all images had to maintain the same percentage ratio). If a larger version of a logo was needed, a new stat had to be shot of it. If a smaller version, likewise. Each new size had to have its turn on the stat camera.

Honestly, this was generally a pretty painless procedure...until you compare it with the reduction/enlargement process on the Macintosh—clicking on an image corner and pulling.

creative firm: **PIRMAN COMMUNICATIONS**
designer: **Brian Pirman**
client: **Pirman Communications**

Each of these stationery pieces requires a slightly different size of logo—two on the letterhead.

130 East Walnut Street Suite 304 Green Bay, WI 54301

130 East
Walnut Street

Suite 304

Green Bay, WI
54301

414·435·9046

Fax/Modem
414·435·9049

creative firm: **GREGG & ASSOCIATES**
designer: **Michael Buster**
client: **Ewing Marrion Kauffman Foundation**

An enlarged, screened logo often makes a good background for business stationery.

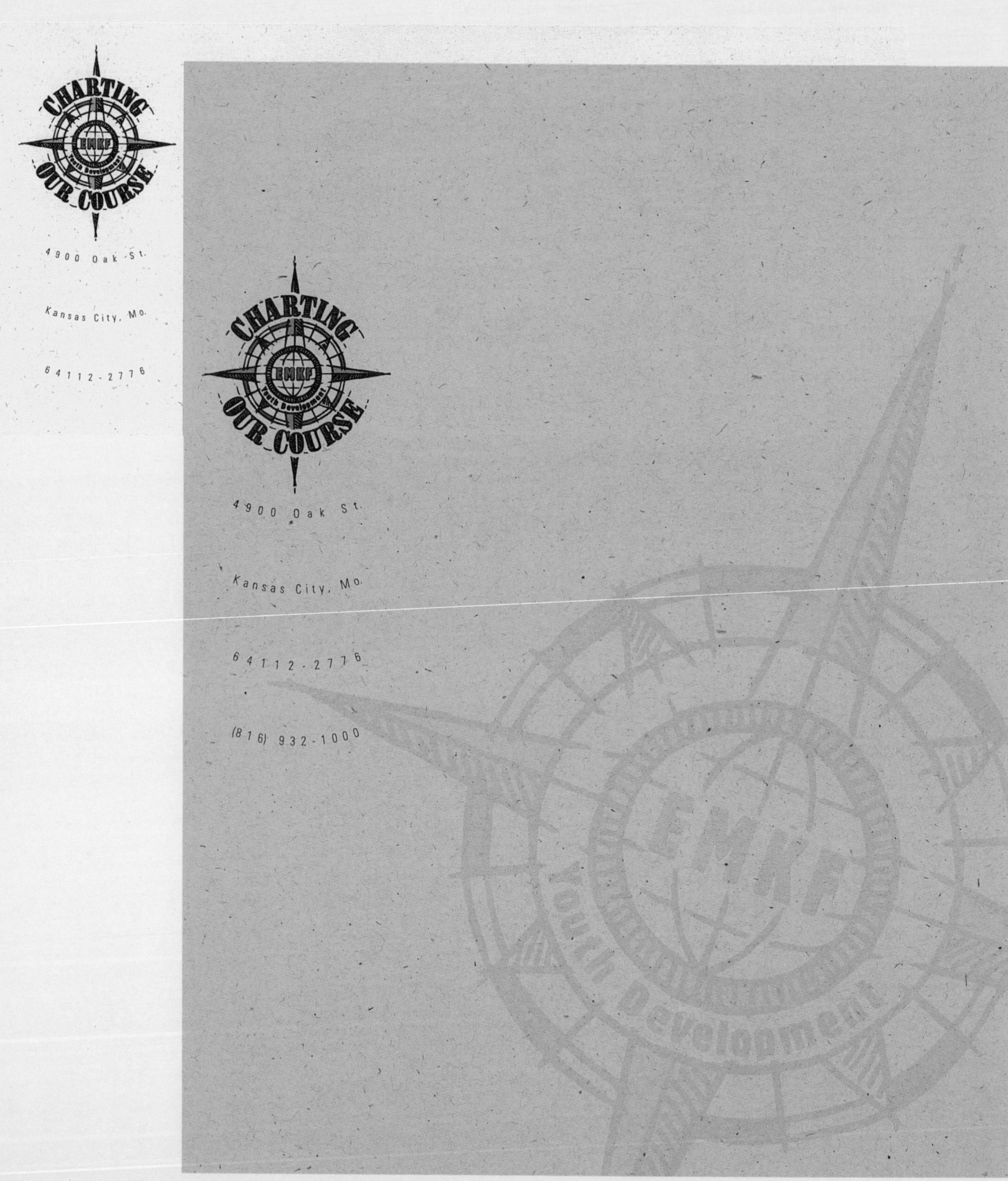

creative firm: WALL-TO-WALL STUDIOS
designers: Bernard Vy, James Nesbitt
client: Telerama

Notice typography was deleted from enlarged logo.

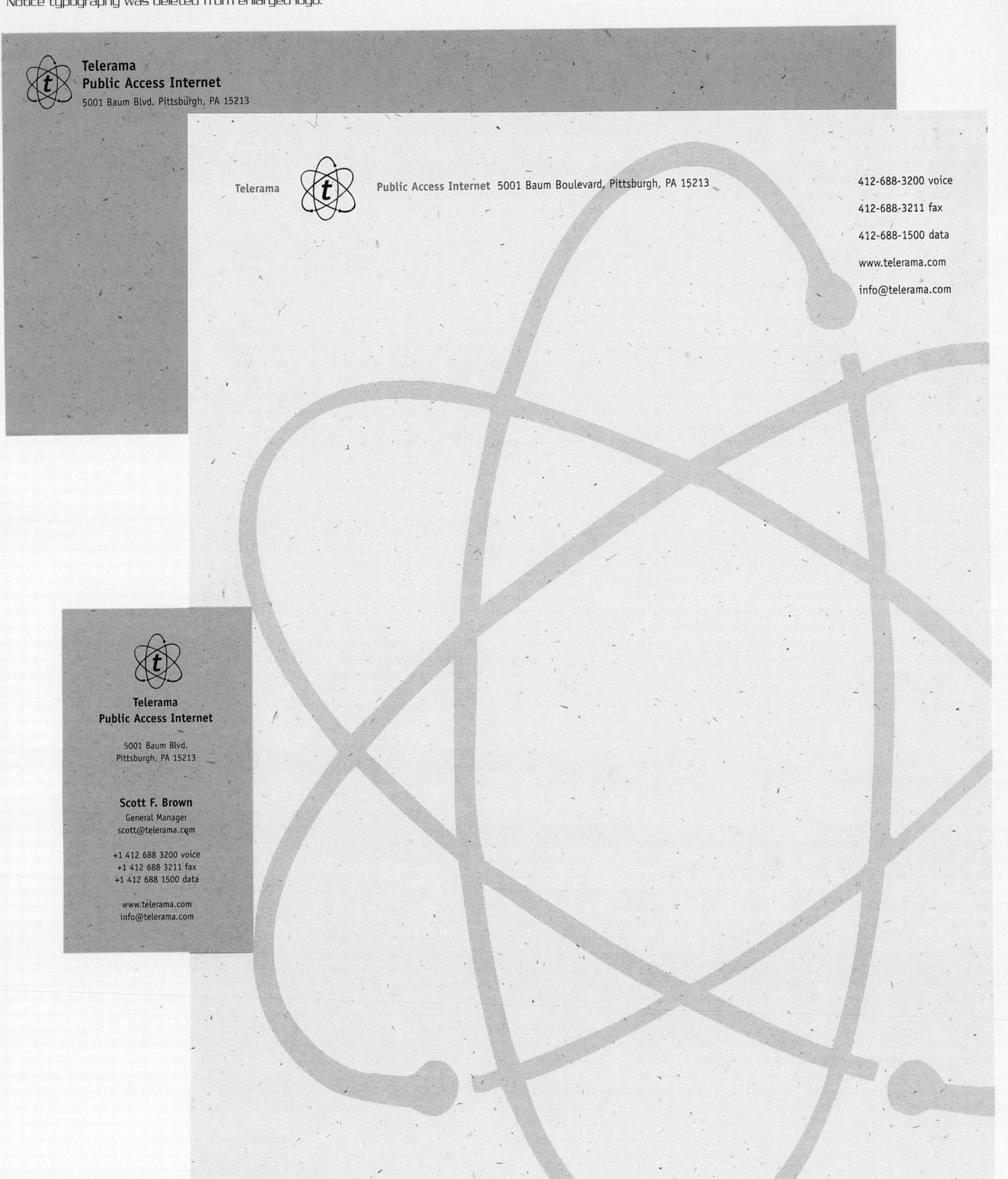

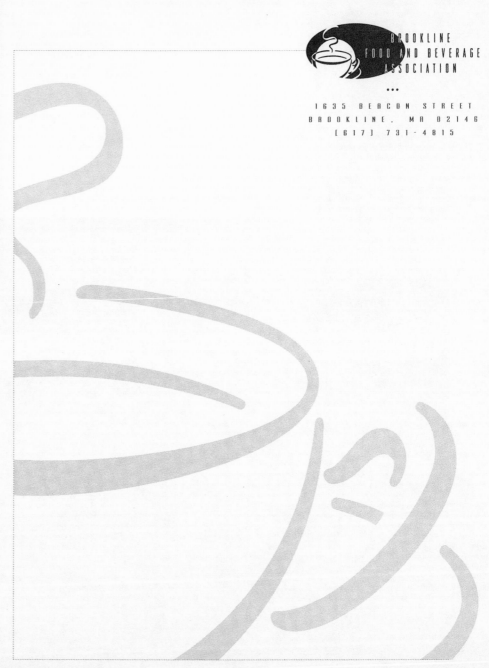

creative firm: **BLACK BEAN STUDIOS**
designer: **Alisha Vera**
client: **Brookline Food & Beverage Association**

Lines from the logo are enlarged and printed on both envelope and letterhead.

BROOKLINE
FOOD AND BEVERAGE
ASSOCIATION

1 6 3 5 B E A C O N S T R E E T
B R O O K L I N E , M A 0 2 1 4 6
[6 1 7] 7 3 1 - 4 8 1 5

creative firm: **STUDIO 405**
designers: **MariAnn Donnelly, Jodi Bloom**
client: **Studio 405**

Iconic logo elements are printed together and separately in various sizes.

studio
405

design

consulting

production

405 aspen street, nw

washington, dc 20012

jodi bloom
principal

405 aspen street, nw
washington, dc 20012

voice
202 723 4011

fax
202 723 1069

e-mail
jodi@studio405.com

web
www.studio405.com

design consulting production

405 aspen street, nw | washington, dc 20012
voice 202 723 4011 *fax* 202 723 1069 *e-mail* info@studio405.com *web* www.studio405.com

creative firm: **HANDLER DESIGN GROUP, INC.**
designer: **Bruce Handler**
client: **Fernando Garcia**

A single element taken from the logo was enlarged and printed as a background in this stationery package.

Fernando Garcia

170-20 Dreiser Loop
Bronx, New York 10475
718-671-8859 Phone
718-671-0864 Fax
7209@mne.com E-Mail

Fernando Garcia
170-20 Dreiser Loop Bronx, New York 10475
718-671-8859 Phone 718-671-0864 Fax 7209@mne.com E-Mail

Fernando Garcia
170-20 Dreiser Loop
Bronx, New York 10475

creative firm: **TILKA DESIGN**
designers: **Carla Mueller, Mark Mularz**
client: **free spirit Publishing**

An image printed in different colors and sizes offers visual interest, but maintains a corporate identity.

400 First Avenue North • Suite 616
Minneapolis, MN 55401-1724

400 First Avenue North • Suite 616 • Minneapolis, MN 55401-1724
phone 612.338.2068 • fax 612.337.5050 • help4kids@freespirit.com

Judy Galbraith
president

400 First Avenue North • Suite 616 • Minneapolis, MN 55401-1724
phone 612.338.2068 • fax 612.337.5050 • help4kids@freespirit.com

creative firm: **INSIGHT DESIGN COMMUNICATIONS**
designers: **Sherrie Holdeman, Tracy Holdeman**
client: **Fresh Paint**

Partial logo is increased in size and printed with a two- or three-sided bleed in a muted color.

Fresh Paint
322 South Mosley
Wichita, Kansas 67202

Fresh Paint
322 South Mosley
Wichita, Kansas 67202
TEL 316-262-6540
FAX 316-262-4656
MOBILE 316-734-3936

Fresh Paint
KIM HILL
322 South Mosley
Wichita, Kansas 67202
TEL 316-262-6540
FAX 316-262-4656
MOBILE 316-734-3936

creative firm: **RANDI MARGRABIA DESIGN**
designer: **Randi Shalit Margrabia**
client: **Historic East Market Street**

Different logo icons are each enlarged and printed on different stationery pieces.

134
Arch
Street
★
Philadelphia
Pennsylvania
19106

Chairman
Lynn Martin Haskin, Ph.D.

Vice Chairman
Marvin D. Ginsberg

Secretary
Robert H. Zimmerman, Esq.

Treasurer
Gerald M. Maier

Board of Directors
Martha B. Aikens
Morton W. Altshuler
William S. Blades
L. Clarke Blynn
Thomas J. Cavanaugh
Joseph F. Coradino
James Cuorato
Walter D'Alessio
Ricardo M. Dunston
Eleanor Gesensway
William A. Kingsley
Ann M. Krupnick
Michelle T. Leonard
Robert Marrone
Stephen P. Mullin
George D. Norton, Esq.
Christopher W. Sayer
Luca Sena
Frank Siefert, A.I.A.
Barry P. Shane
Rick Snyderman
Stanley F. Taraila
John E. Taxin
James A. Trimble
Joseph C. Vignola
Richard R. Zeghibe

Executive Director
Janet Holmes

134
Arch
Street
★
Philadelphia, PA
19106
★
Telephone
215·440·9166
Fax
215·440·0793

134
Arch
Street
★
Philadelphia
Pennsylvania
19106
★
Telephone
215·440·9166
Fax
215·440·0793

creative firm: **FUSZION ART + DESIGN**
designers: **Richard Lee Heffner, Anthony Fletcher, Michael A. Pfister**
client: **FUSZION Art + Design**

Artwork printed in various sizes maintains continuity throughout this stationery. Printed negatively on the back of letterheads, a watermark effect is created.

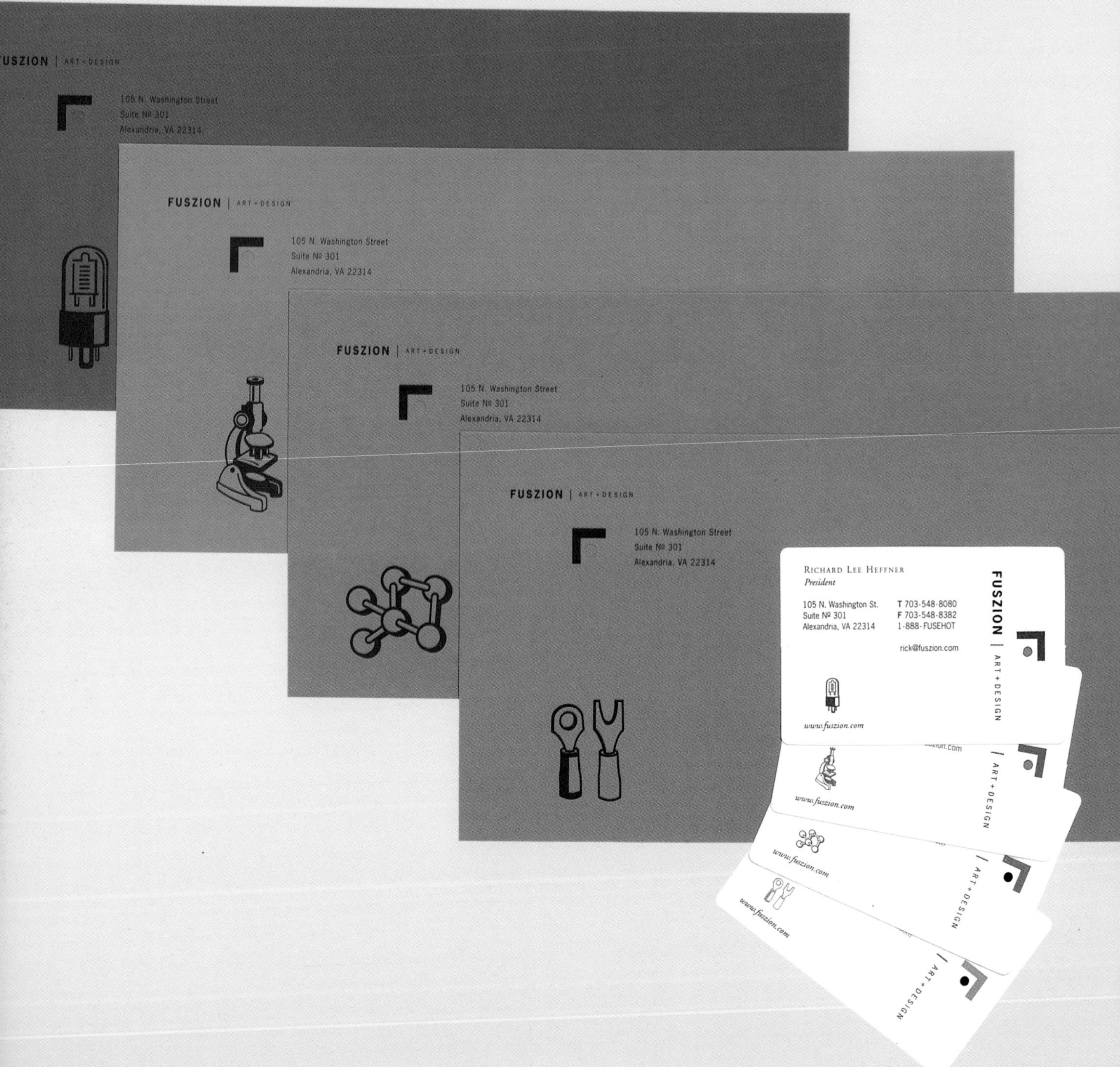

FUSZION | ART + DESIGN
105 N. Washington Street
Suite № 301
Alexandria, VA 22314
T 703-548-8080
F 703-548-8382
1-888-FUSEHOT
www.fuszion.com
fu • szion (fyü-shən) n. (1997)
a synthesis of creative energy and marketing insight to create compelling visual communications.

creative firm: MUIR AGENCY
designer: Bernard Sandoval
client: Broadmoor Skating Club

Script letter makes an elegant background when enlarged and screened.

BROADMOOR SKATING CLUB

creative firm: ELLIOTT VAN DEUTSCH
designers: Rachel Deutsch, Erika Maxwell
client: Net Impact Systems, Inc.

Typographical logo element printed in a paler color than original produces consistency across this system.

Net Impact Systems, Inc.
103 West Broad Street @ Suite 100 @ Falls Church, VA 22046
(703) 534-8900 @ FAX: (703) 534-8934

@
Net Impact Systems, Inc.
@
103 West Broad Street
@
Suite 100
@
Falls Church, VA 22046

Net Impact Systems, Inc.
@
103 West Broad Street
@
Suite 100
@
Falls Church, VA 22046
@
(703) 534-8900
@
FAX: (703) 534-8934
@
www.BestAnswer.com

The @nswer Is The Object

creative firm: **FUNK & ASSOCIATES**
designer: **Beverly Soasey**
client: **Marché**

Screened fruit printed in the background at different sizes makes a successful and appropriate image for this café.

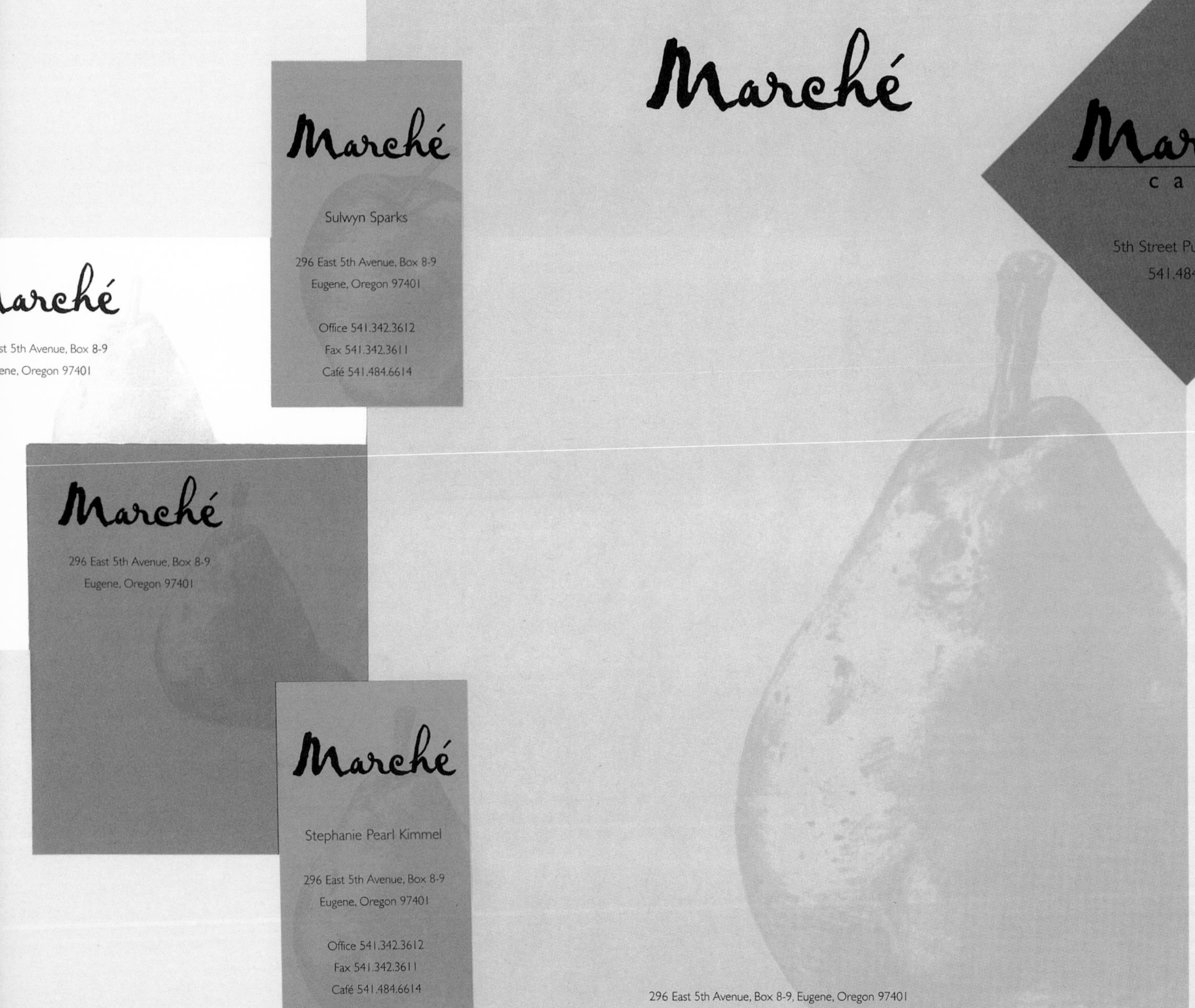

Marché
Marché
Sulwyn Sparks
296 East 5th Avenue, Box 8-9
Eugene, Oregon 97401
Office 541.342.3612
Fax 541.342.3611
Café 541.484.6614
arché
ast 5th Avenue, Box 8-9
gene, Oregon 97401
Mar
caf
5th Street Pub
541.484.
Marché
296 East 5th Avenue, Box 8-9
Eugene, Oregon 97401
Marché
Stephanie Pearl Kimmel
296 East 5th Avenue, Box 8-9
Eugene, Oregon 97401
Office 541.342.3612
Fax 541.342.3611
Café 541.484.6614
296 East 5th Avenue, Box 8-9, Eugene, Oregon 97401
Phone 541.342.3612 ◆ Fax 541.342.3611

Design has always had a firm foundation in geometry, even if it just means working on a grid. Is it even necessary to mention the difficulty in producing perfect geometric figures by hand? Ovals are closer to impossible in execution than circles are. Squares, rectangles, and triangles are easier, but still involve perfectly straight lines, precision angles, and corners that meet exactly. And those are just the simple shapes! There is no question that the computer offers superior control when dealing with geometric perfection.

creative firm: SAYLES GRAPHIC DESIGN
designer: John Sayles
client: Hotel Pattee

Perfect right angles are absolutely necessary when using several rectangular and square shapes together.

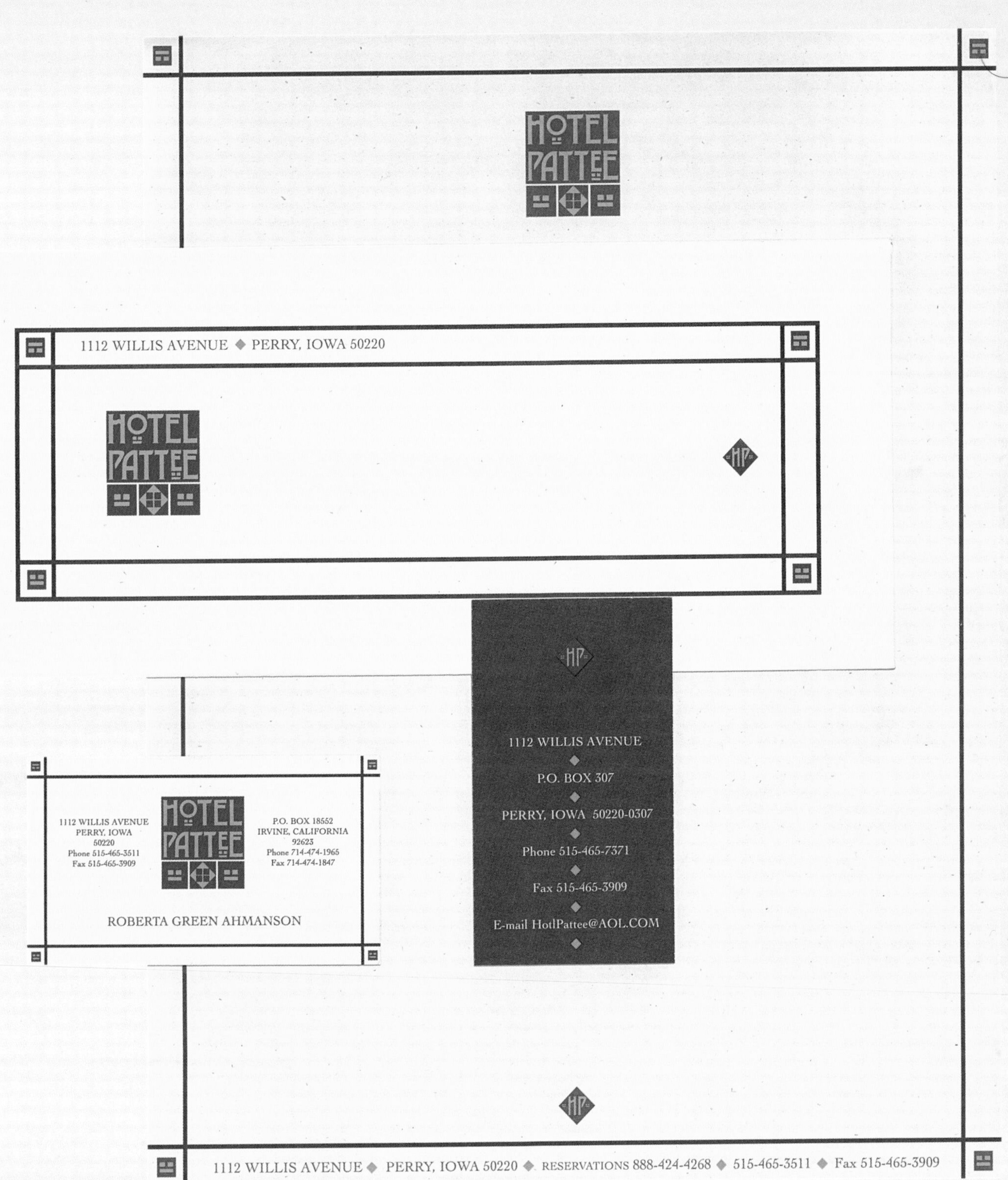

creative firm: **McELVENEY & PALOZZI DESIGN GROUP, INC.**
designers: Jonathan Westfall, William McElveney, Stephen Palozzi
client: McElveney & Palozzi Design Group, Inc.

An exceptionally well-done logo of geometric strength has all kinds of three-dimensional feel.

1255 University Avenue - Suite 200
Rochester, New York 14607

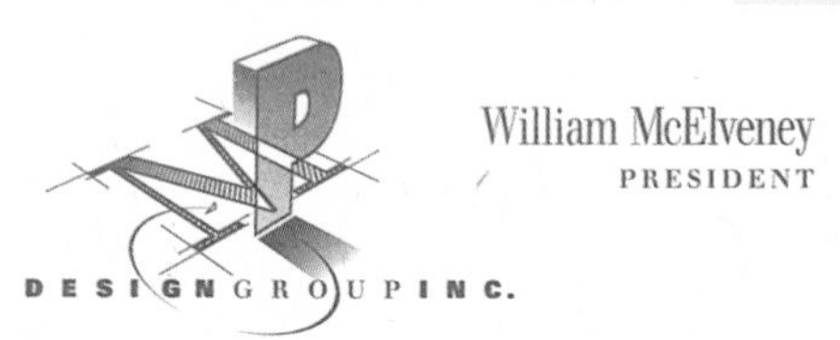

McElveney&Palozzi
1255 University Avenue - Suite 200 . Rochester, New York 14607
Phone (716) 473-7630 . Fax (716) 473-9506
e-mail: mnp@frontiernet.net

McElveney&Palozzi

1255 University Avenue - Suite 200 . Rochester, New York 14607 . Phone (716) 473-7630 . Fax (716) 473-9506
e-mail: mnp@frontiernet.net

creative firm: DESIGN MOVES, LTD.
designers: Laurie Medeiros Freed, Amy Forbes Bunting
client: Clarity Consulting

This logo has a nice repetitive-curve relationship between two open ovals represented as "C"s.

creative firm: **X DESIGN COMPANY**
designers: **Alex Valderrama, Kay Flierl**
client: **X Design Company**

Flame-like rays extending from a basic 360º (circle) shape are much easier to execute in a computer file than by hand.

2525 West Main Street, Suite 201 x Littleton, CO 80120

fn 303.797.6311 fx 303.797.6481

2525 West Main Street
Suite 201
Littleton, CO 80120

kay flierl

fn 303.797.6311
fx 303.797.6481

[design made fresh daily]

creative firm: HORNALL ANDERSON DESIGN WORKS, INC.
designers: Jack Anderson, David Bates
client: Hornall Anderson Design Works, Inc.

This logo, comprised of most of the basic three-dimensional shapes, is a great study in space relations.

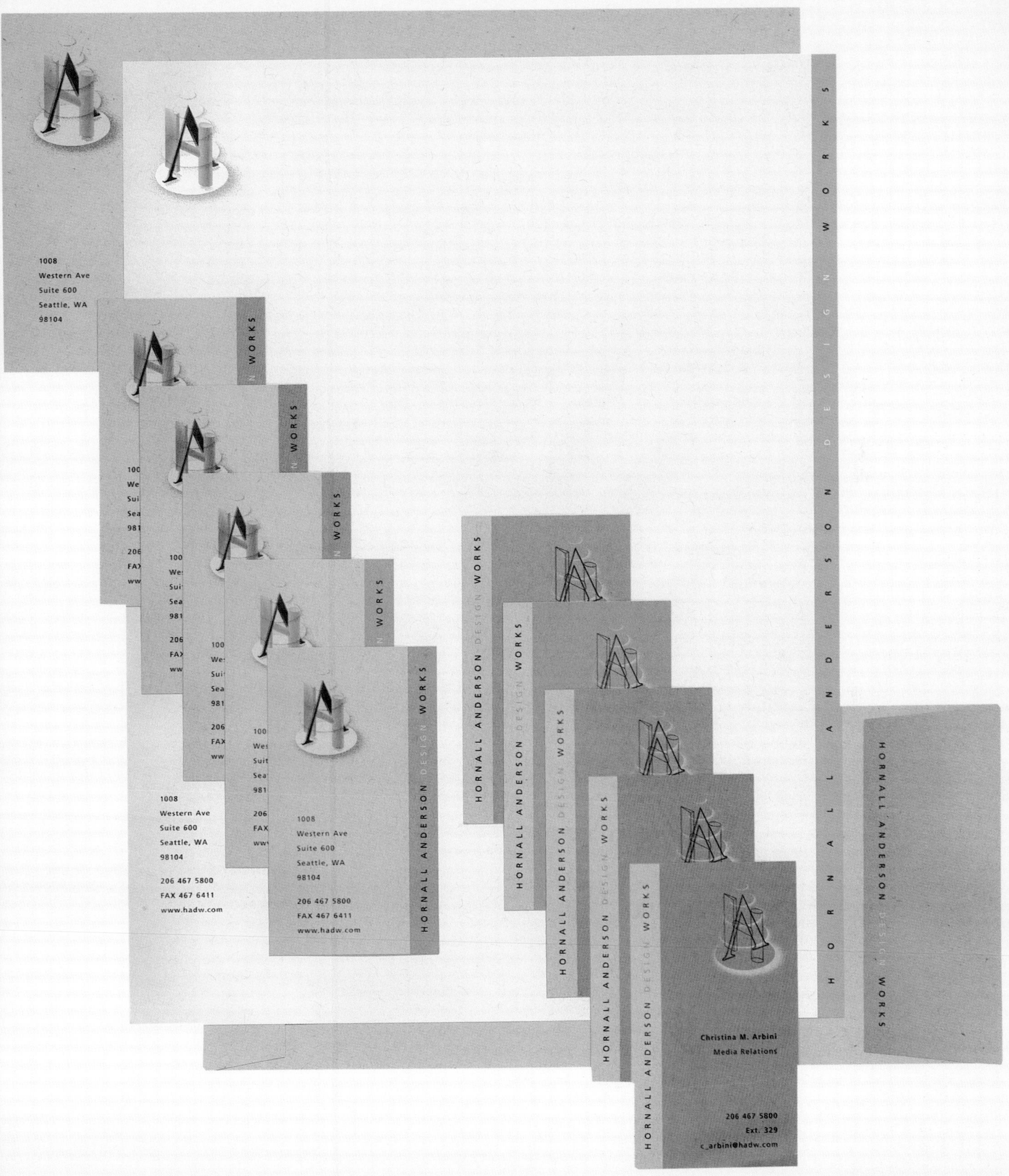

creative firm: **SPANGLER DESIGN TEAM**
designers: **Jeff Spry, Mark Spangler**
client: **Spangler Design Team**

Perfectly-spaced rays emanating from 360° are just a click away on the computer.

creative firm: **DESIGN ASSOCIATES**
designers: **Kathy Kruse, Leslie Snodgrass**
client: **Design Associates**

Any shape with specific angles should always be produced via computer.

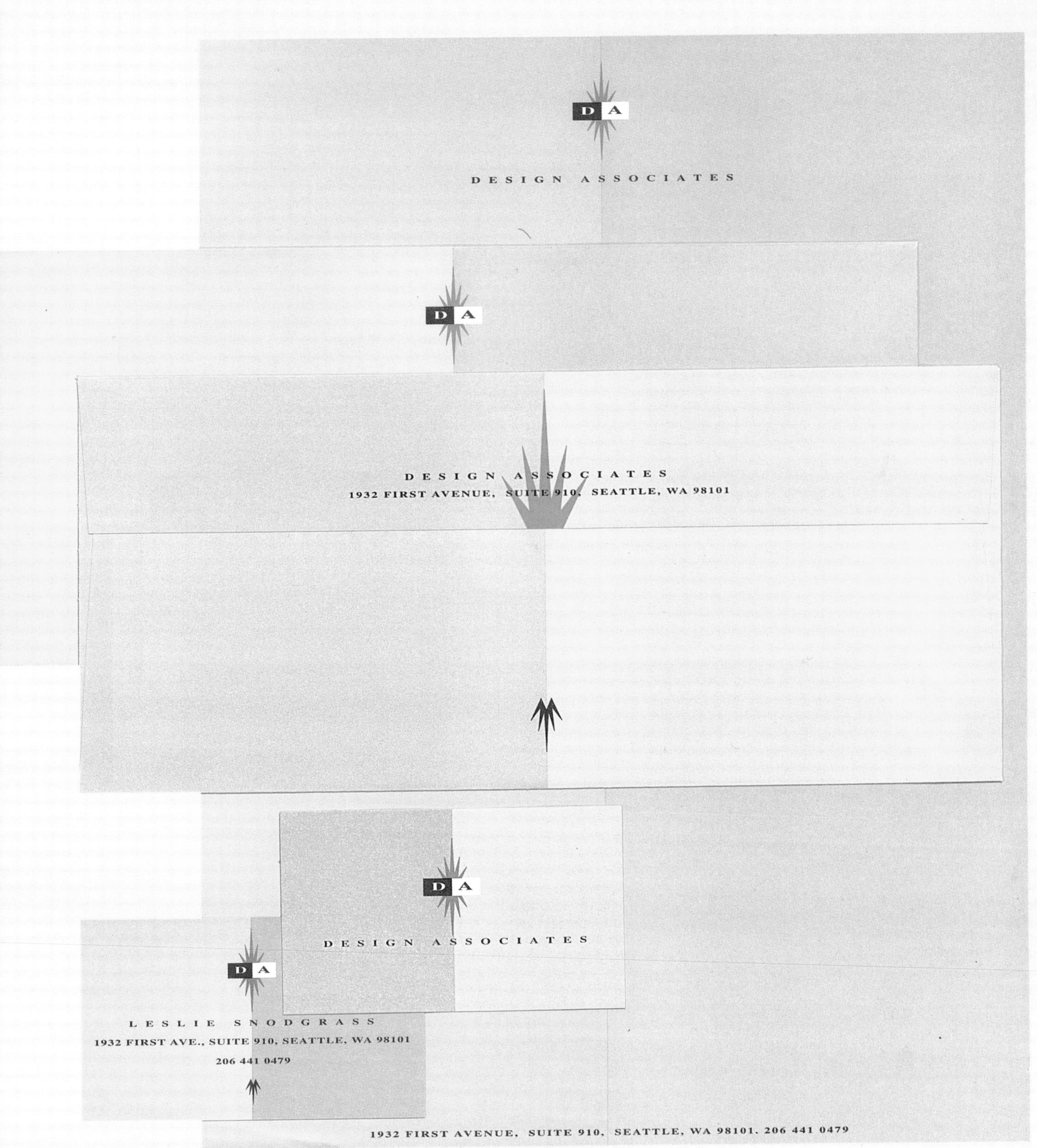

creative firm: **ART O MAT DESIGN**
designers: **Jacki McCarthy, Mark Kaufman**
client: **Technology Alliance**

Perfect spacing and alignment are easily-accessible features of computer design.

creative firm: **LAT DISEÑO GRÁFICO**
designer: **Lydimarie Aponte Tañoñ**
client: **CAM Services, Inc./Common Area Maintenance, Inc.**

Geometrically-balanced positive and negative shapes would be very difficult to measure and draw.

PO Box 29789
San Juan PR 00929-0789

Juan R. Marrero, P.E.

PO Box 29789
San Juan PR 00929-0789
Tel 787.756.5176
Fax 787.765.2557
Beeper 250.0140 u.123.5650

PO Box 29789 San Juan PR 00929-0789 Tel 787.756.5176 Fax 787.765.2557

creative firm: **TACKETT-BARBARIA DESIGN**
designer: **Steve Barbaria**
client: **Global Guardian**

Ovals, and shapes based on ovals, have always been very difficult to get just right when working by hand.

Global Guardian

Global Guardian USA, Inc.

Steven A. Minor
Vice President
Industry Relations

PO Box 437
Key Biscayne, Florida 33149
Phone: 305.365.0423
FAX: 305.361.3503

Global Guardian

creative firm: Gr8
designers: Morton Jackson, Tim Thompson, Chuck Seelye
client: Gr8

The superiority of computer design really shines with three-dimensional framework.

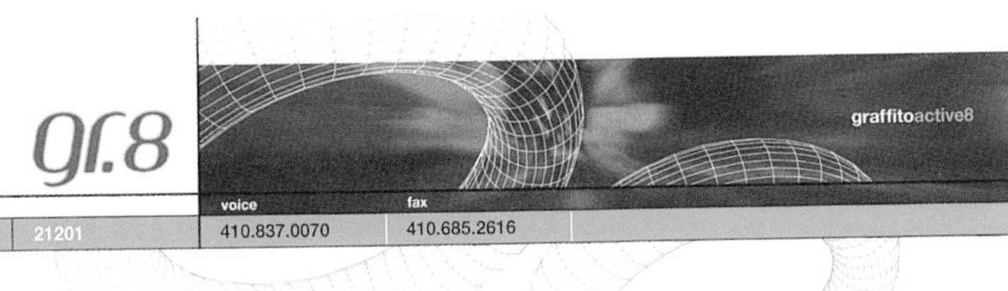

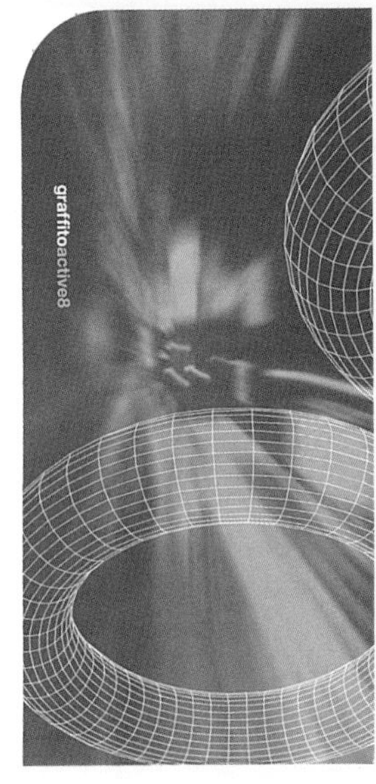

creative firm: **GARRY ALAN DESIGN, INC.**
designers: **Jay Maurico, Kathy Spies, Garry Weiner**
client: **Genesis Cable Systems, L.L.C.**

Futuristic, hard-edged logos are a natural outlet of computer design.

7701 95th Street
P.O. Box 0383
Pleasant Prairie, WI
53158-0383

7701 95th Street
P.O. Box 0383
Pleasant Prairie, WI
53158-0383

Voice 414 947 0720
Toll Free 800 222 0060
Fax 414 947 0724

genesis cable systems, l.l.c.

securing the future

genesis cable systems, l.l.c.

7701 95th Street
P.O. Box 0383
Pleasant Prairie, WI
53158-0383

Voice 414 947 0720
Toll Free 800 222 0060
Fax 414 947 0724

jim coleman *c.e.o*

creative firm: ARIAS ASSOCIATES
designers: Maurico Arias, Steve Mortensen, Stephanie Yee
client: Release Software

Gradients aid in the illusion of dimensionality of geometrically-drawn shapes.

RELEASE
SOFTWARE

100 Independence Drive Menlo Park, CA 94025-1113 Tel 650.833.0200 Fax 650.833.0213 www.releasesoft.com

creative firm: **MURRELL DESIGN GROUP**
designer: **Lotte Winkel**
client: **Enerlight**

Images with a base in Fibonacci numbers are surely simpler produced on Macintosh.

creative firm: GR8
designers: Morton Jackson, Rob Rhinehart
client: Fortner Software

Shapes finding their origins in the oval often suggest orbits and, necessarily, very modern or cutting edge businesses.

bill rigney
vice president
marketing &
channel development

bill@fortner.com
http://www.fortner.com

Fortner Software LLC
100 Carpenter Drive
Sterling, VA 20164

[703]478.0181 x117 [703]689.9593 fax

news release

http://www.fortner.com

Fortner Software LLC
100 Carpenter Dr
Sterling, VA 20164

[703] 478.0181 [703] 689.9593 fax

creative firm: POLLMAN MARKETING ARTS, INC.
designers: Jennifer Pollman
client: MasterPrint

A sun formed in the Gestalt of geometric elements could be produced by hand, but those increments of degrees are so simple on the computer!

MASTERPRINT

3400 INDUSTRIAL LANE #2

BROOMFIELD

COLORADO 80020

TEL: 303 . 466 . 1800

FAX: 303 . 438 . 8454

http://www.masterprnt.com

creative firm: **PUSH**
designers: **Steve Barretto, Todd Foreman**
client: **Production Resources, Inc., Sausalito CA.**

Simple shapes offer a very clean logo.

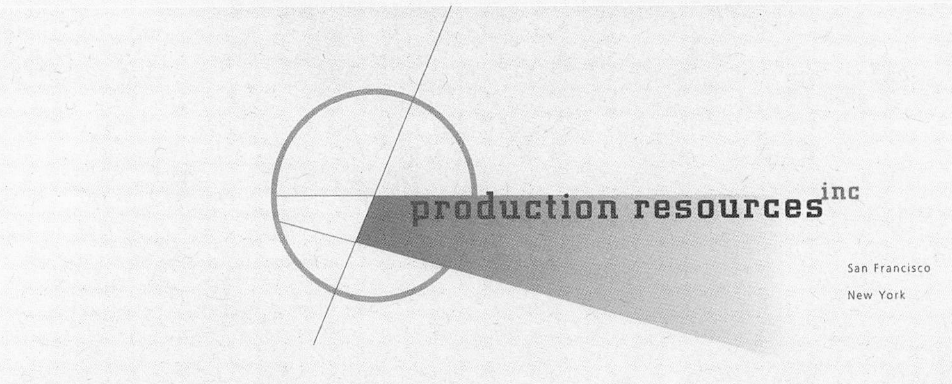

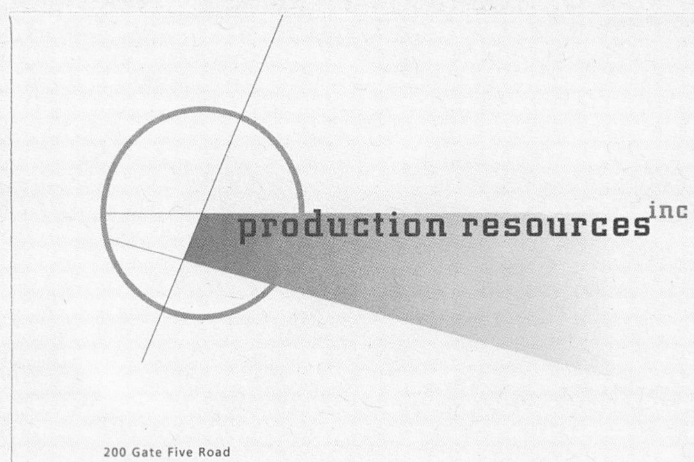

415 289 7510 tel 415 289 7515 fax
Production Resources Inc. 200 Gate Five Road, Suite 101 Sausalito, CA 94965

Do I really need to expound on the positive aspects of copy-and-paste? Compared to handwork, it's almost ridiculously easy to duplicate, change colors, change orientation, or change sizes. Designers can practice all day seeing how very minute differences effect an overall project—which may or may not be a good thing. It's great to have all the options, but there seemed to be more preplanning of a design before the computer revolution.

creative firm: LYNN SCHULTE DESIGN
designer: Lynn Schulte
client: Judy MacManus

Obviously a Cary Grant fan!

creative firm: PUSH
designers: John Barretto, Steve Barretto, Todd Foreman
client: Schneider/Swinks Photography

After the final version was created, this eye image was easy to duplicate, size, and turn.

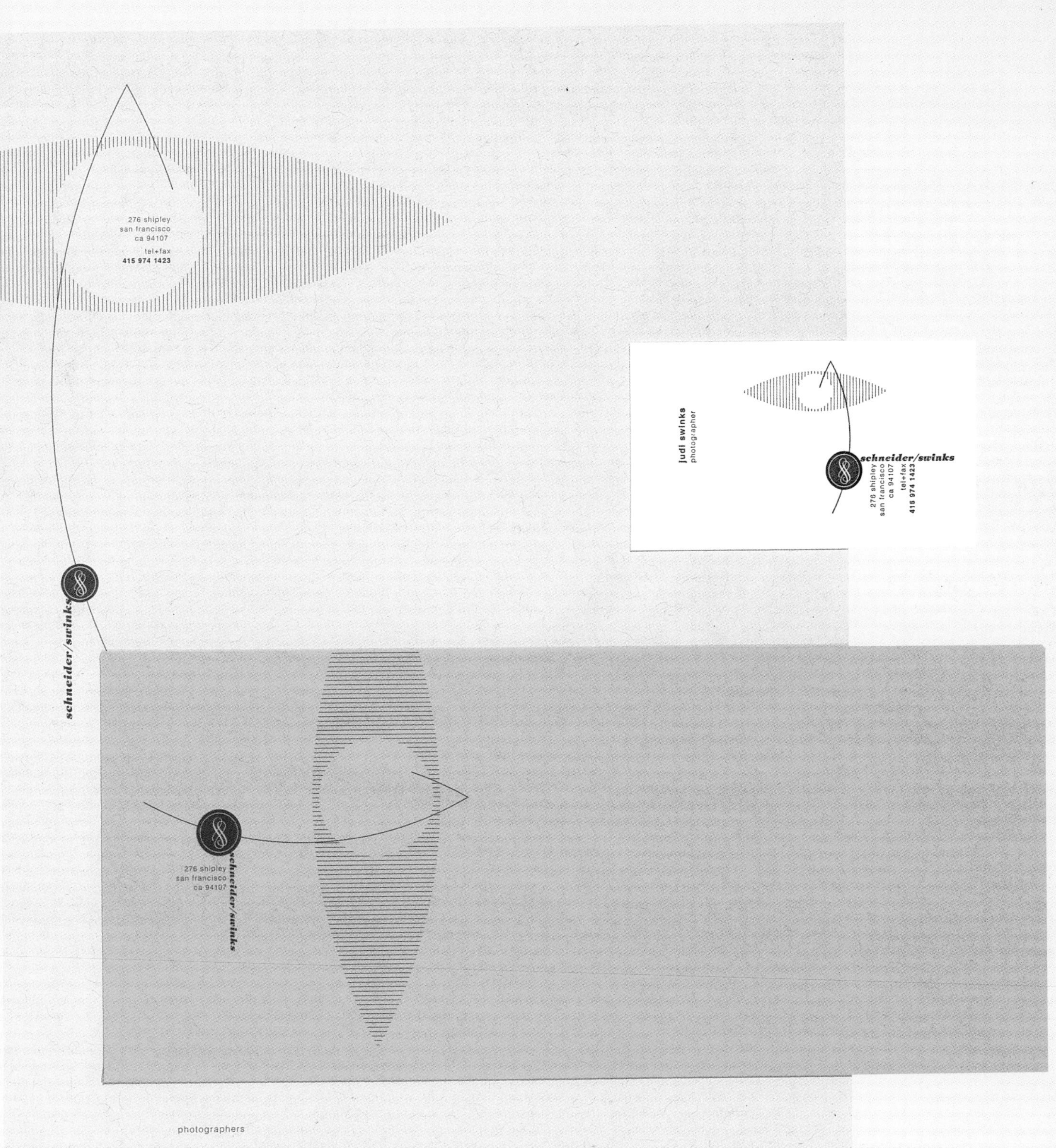

creative firm: **1-EARTH GRAPHICS**
designer: **Lisa Harris**
client: **Tri-County Board of Recovery & Mental Health Services**

Creating one figure and copying it takes less time and effort than creating three.

405 Public Square ▪ Suite 330 ▪ Troy, OH 45373 ▪ (937) 335-7727 ▪ 1-800-589-2853 ▪ FAX (937) 335-8816

405 Public Square ▪ Suite 330 ▪ Troy, OH 45373

DAVID MATHEWS, Ph.D.

EXECUTIVE DIRECTOR

405 Public Square ▪ Suite 330 ▪ Troy, OH 45373
TEL (937) 335-7727 Ext. 13 ▪ 1-800-589-2853 ▪ FAX (937) 335-8816
E-MAIL mathews@erinet.com

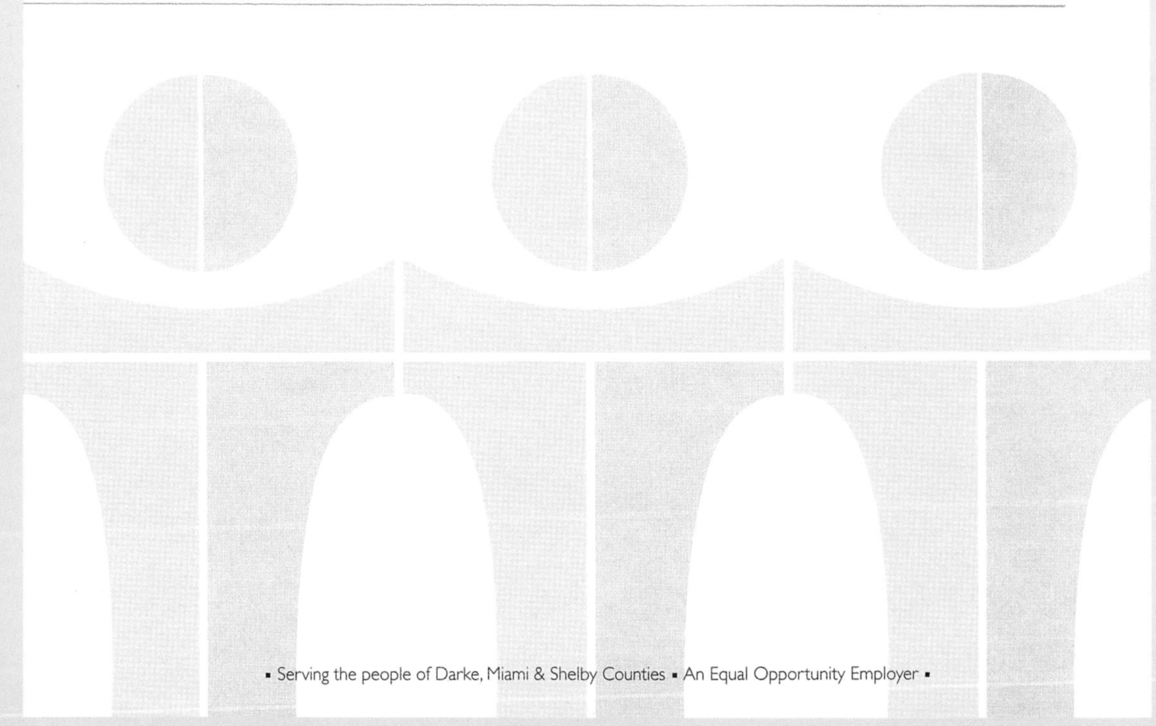

creative firm: **WINDIGO**
designers: **James B. Gubelmann, Janet M. Ralli**
client: **Seven Seas International, Ltd.**

Besides just duplicating elements, the computer allows the designer to work with placement options until the repeated objects are in perfect relation with one another.

SEVEN SEAS
INTERNATIONAL, LTD

730 Fifth Avenue, 9th floor,
New York, NY 10019

PHONE: 212-333-8796
FAX: 212-307-3198
EMAIL: MGubelmann@aol.com

SEVEN SEAS
INTERNATIONAL, LTD

730 Fifth Avenue, 9th floor,
New York, NY 10019

SEVEN SEAS
INTERNATIONAL, LTD

Marjorie B. Gubelmann
President

730 Fifth Avenue, 9th floor,
New York, NY 10019

PHONE: 212-333-8796
FAX: 212-307-3198
EMAIL: MGubelmann@aol.com

creative firm: **WENDY QUESINBERRY DESIGN**
designer: **Wendy Quesinberry**
client: **Roxbury Chiropractic**

Making a pattern from a logo element is a much speeded process on the computer.

creative firm: AIRE DESIGN COMPANY
designers: David Kolb, Shari Rykowski, Matthew Rivera
client: aire design company

Repeated and overlapping outlines and text create a sense of motion and vitality.

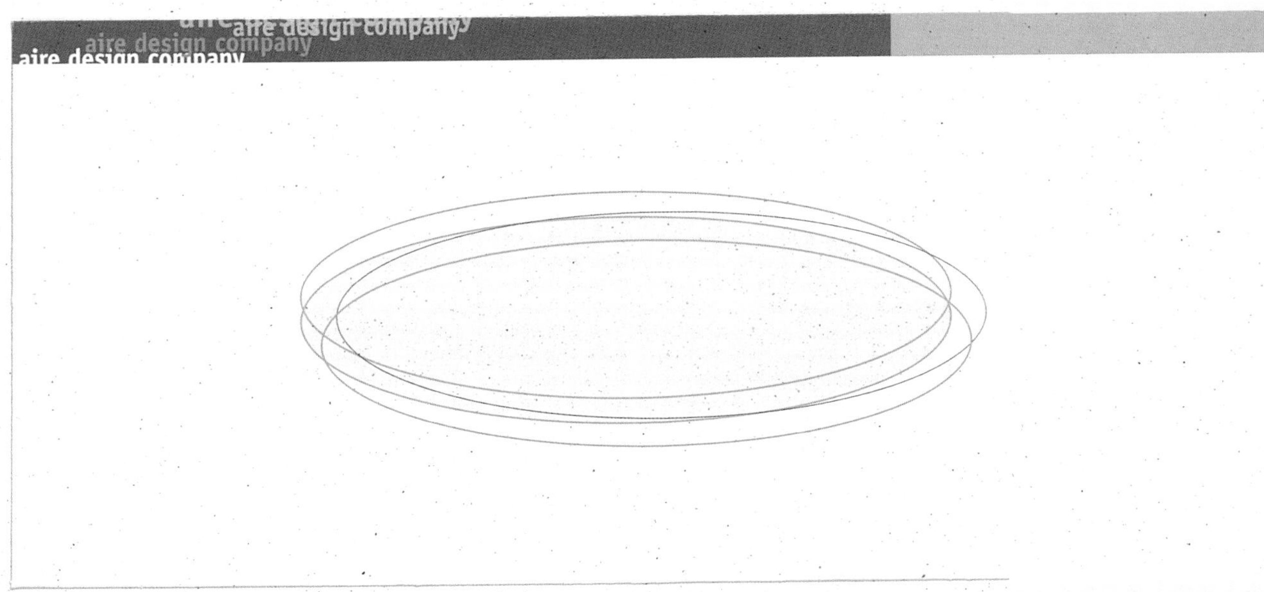

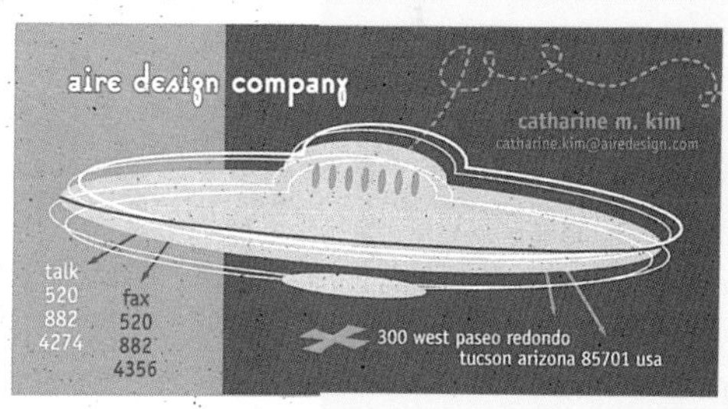

300 west paseo redondo
tucson arizona 85701 usa
talk: 520 882 4274
fax: 520 882 4356
email: aire.mail@airedesign.com

Exploring the topic of textures with regard to computer use and creation is certainly too broad to fully cover here. Suffice it to say there are numerous manners in which to produce or use a texture as the following pages will demonstrate.

creative firm: **BRD DESIGN**
designer: **Peter King Robbins**
client: **Orduna Design**

Beautiful texture is printed in differing intensities and focuses.

ORDUÑA
DESIGN

ORDUÑA
DESIGN

ORDUÑA
DESIGN
307 South Robertson Blvd.
Beverly Hills, CA 90211
307 South Robertson Blvd. Beverly Hills, C
phone 310.358.9670 fax 310.358.9629

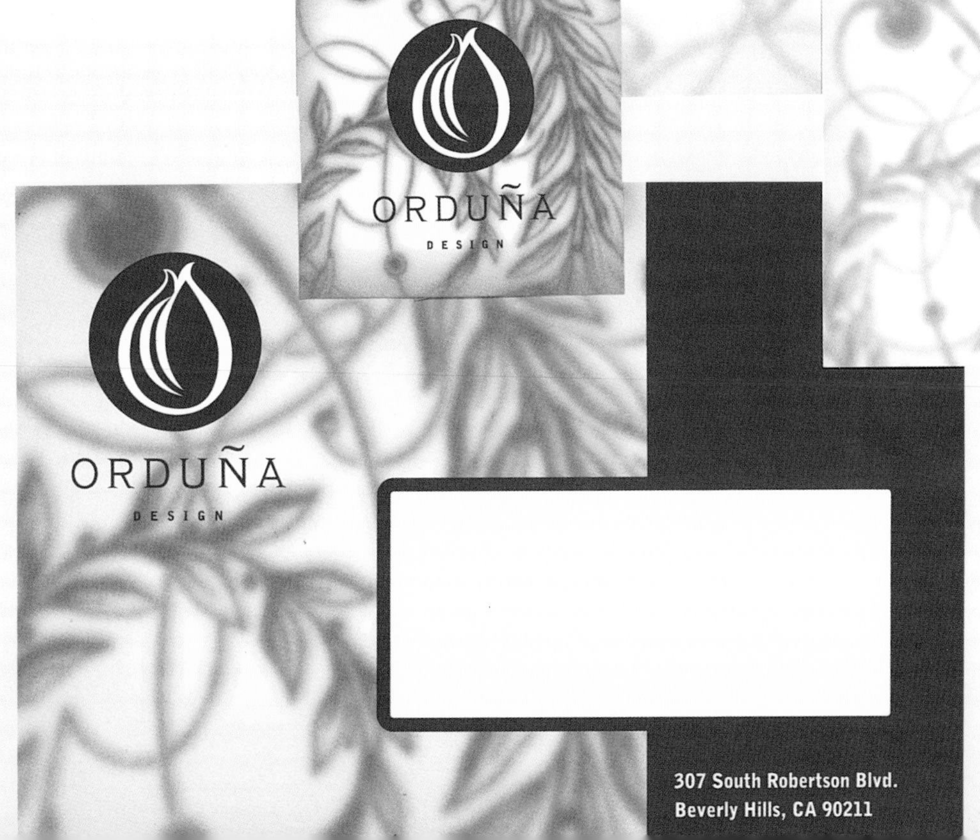
ORDUÑA
DESIGN
ORDUÑA
DESIGN
307 South Robertson Blvd.
Beverly Hills, CA 90211

creative firm: **CONNELLY DESIGN, INC.**
designer: **Dennis Scheible**
client: **Transitions**

Texture composed of diamonds in transition is very appropriate for business named "Transitions".

200 West Madison Street
Suite 2500
Chicago, Illinois 60606-3440

200 West Madison Street
Suite 2500
Chicago, Illinois 60606-3440

Denise Reardon
President

Office 312.855.5300
Direct Line 312.368.5829
Toll Free 800.621.9909
Fax 312.368.1490

200 West Madison Street • Suite 2500 • Chicago, Illinois 60606-3440
312.855.5300 • Fax 312.368.5857
An affiliate of Baird & Warner

creative firm: FROGDESIGN TEAM
designer: frogdesign team
client: Dillingham Consulting

The size change of dots in an exaggerated screen texture add visual interest.

dillinghamconsulting

Organization &
Team Development

428 Palmer Avenue
Aptos, CA 95003

tel 408 662·9322
fax 408 662·0122
pdilli@aol.com

dillinghamconsulting

Organization &
Team Development

428 Palmer Avenue
Aptos, CA 95003

creative firm: **G.H. BAILEY COMPANY**
designer: **Gwen Hagaman**
client: **Pure Light/Pure Passion**

Fantastic texture representing light, passion, and laser art.

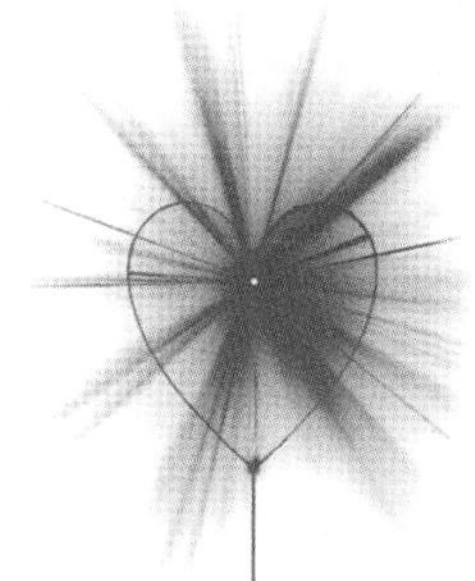

creative firm: PROFILE DESIGN
designers: Thomas McNulty, Brian Jacobson, Jeanne Namkung
client: Mariani Nut Company

Slightly abstract nuts form negative space in a gradient background texture.

709 Dutton Street
P.O Box 808
Winters, CA 95694

John G. Aguiar

709 Dutton Street
P.O Box 808
Winters, CA 95694
Tel 916.795.3311
Fax 916.795.2681

creative firm: **GREG WELSH DESIGN**
designer: **Greg Welsh**
client: **Northward Construction**

Some textures are available on CD or disk.

creative firm: GRAPHICS 2
designer: Kathleen Feeney, Colleen Feeney
client: Chipley Construction, LLC

Scanning photos and adjusting the scan in a photo manipulation program is one way to get an original texture.

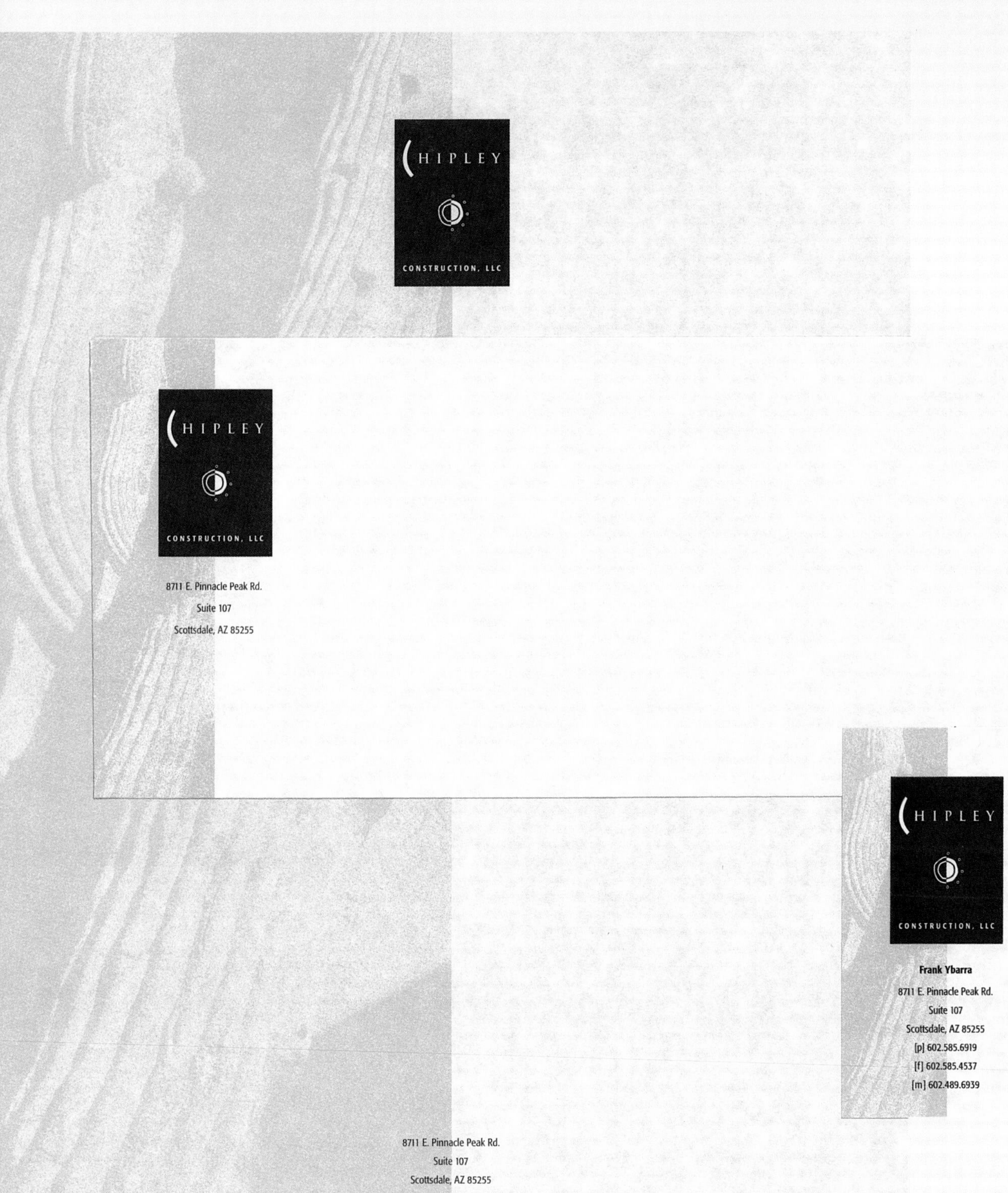

creative firm: **GRAPHICA**
designer: **Al Hidalgo**
client: **Pacchia**

Melting and merging dots form a banded texture for this letterhead.

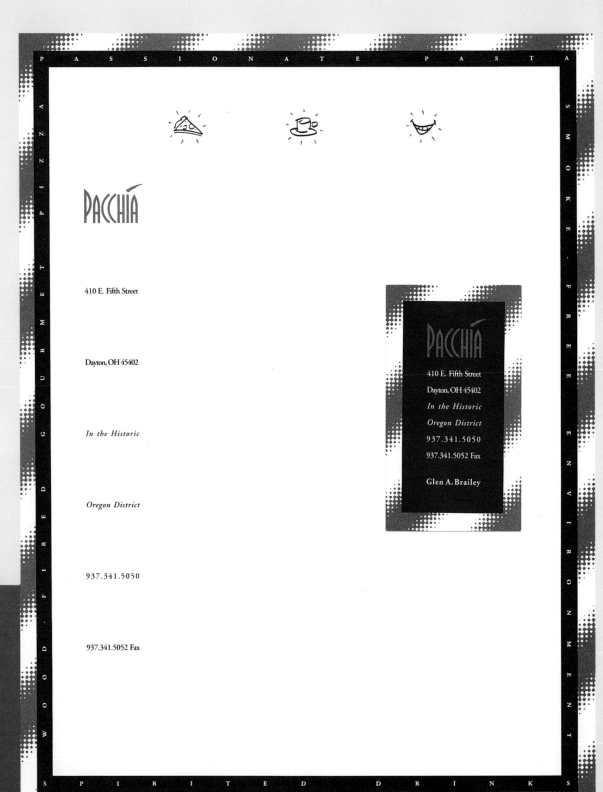

PASSIONATE PASTA SMOKE-FREE ENVIRONMENT SPIRITED DRINKS WOOD-FIRED GOURMET PIZZA

PACCHIA

410 E. Fifth Street

Dayton, OH 45402

In the Historic

Oregon District

937.341.5050

937.341.5052 Fax

PACCHIA
410 E. Fifth Street
Dayton, OH 45402
In the Historic
Oregon District
937.341.5050
937.341.5052 Fax
Glen A. Brailey

PACCHIA
410 E. Fifth Street
Dayton, OH 45402
In the Historic
Oregon District

creative firm: **ENVIRONMENTAL COMMUNICATIONS ASSOCIATES, INC.**
designer: **Traci Schalow, AJ Grant**
client: **PACE**

Textures aren't limited to backgrounds, but can be design elements on their own as the borders show below.

Partners For A
Clean Environment
P.O.Box 791
Boulder, CO 80306

A Program of the City of Boulder, Boulder County, Boulder Chamber of Commerce and Boulder Energy Conservation Center

A Program of the City of Boulder, Boulder County, Boulder Chamber of Commerce and Boulder Energy Conservation Center

Partners For A
Clean Environment
P.O.Box 791
Boulder, CO 80306
Ph: 303-786-PACE
Fx: 303-441-4367

creative firm: **COMPASS DESIGN**
designers: **Mitchell Lindgren, Rich McGowen, Tom Arthur**
client: **Metropolitan Hodder Group**

On this and the next two pages are examples of a stationery system that was designed with different backgrounds/textures, effecting different corporate images with each.

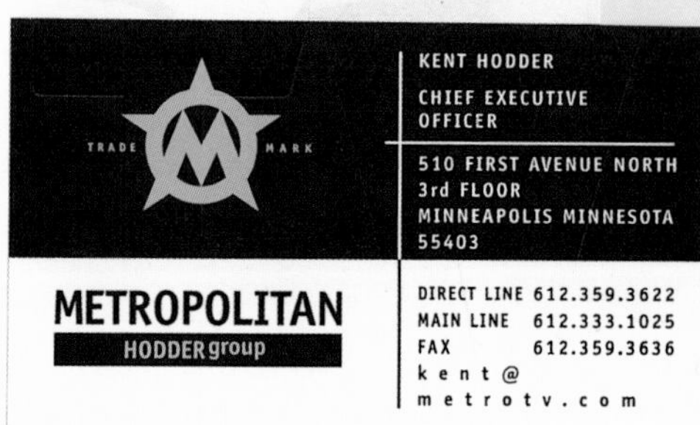

group @
metrotv.com
510 FIRST AVENUE N. 3rd FLOOR
METROPOLITAN
HODDER group
MINNEAPOLIS MINNESOTA 55403
612.333.1025
FAX.359.3636

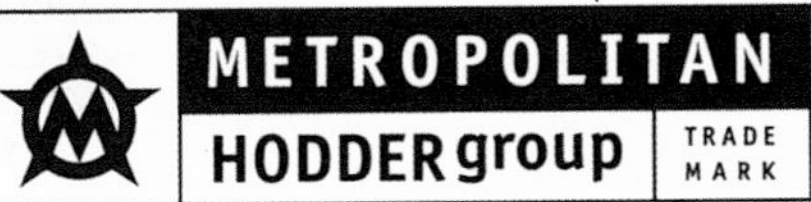

RST AVENUE NORTH 3rd FLOOR MINNEAPOLIS

PRINTED IN U.S.A.

510 FIRST AVENUE N. 3rd FLOOR
MINNEAPOLIS MINNESOTA 55403

612.333.1025
FAX.359.3636

TRADE
MARK
TV

o m

group @
metrotv.com
510 FIRST AVENUE N. 3rd FLOOR
METROPOLITAN
HODDER group
MINNEAPOLIS MINNESOTA 55403
612.333.1025
FAX.359.3636

Some design images are derived directly from computers or computer use and would have simply had no meaning if weren't for the technology we share today.

creative firm: **AFTER HOURS DESIGN & ADVERTISING**
designer: **Beth Shott**
client: **After Hours Design & Advertising**

Would there have been drawings of computers if there were no computers?

16933 SHINEDALE DRIVE
CANYON COUNTRY, CA 91351
PHONE 805.251.0197
FAX 805.251.0625

BETH SHOTT
16933 SHINEDALE DRIVE
CANYON COUNTRY, CA 91351
805.251.0197 / FAX 805.251.0625

AFTER HOURS
DESIGN▸ADVERTISING
16933 SHINEDALE DRIVE
CANYON COUNTRY, CA 91351

creative firm: **ROBERT MEYERS COMMUNICATION DESIGN & PLANNING**
designer: **Robert Meyers**
client: **Indianer Computer Corporation**

This computer corporation uses artwork resembling a circuit board for the back of its stationery pieces. The envelope is silver plastic, looking very much like a magnetic protective covering. Great!

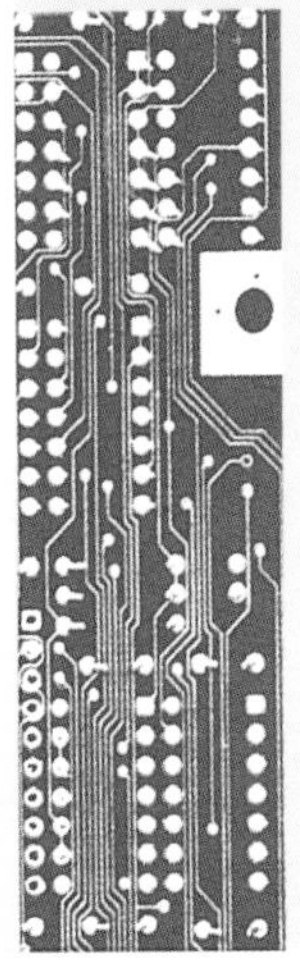

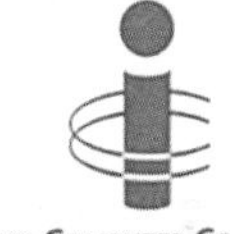

INDIANER COMPUTER CORPORATION

Evan Indianer

(412) 338-3358
Fax: (412) 338-6636
E-Mail: evan@indianer.com
3127 Penn Avenue
Pittsburgh, Pennsylvania
15201

creative firm: **WES GARLATZ GRAPHIC DESIGN**
designer: **Wes Garlatz**
client: **Functional Solutions Group**

Binary code is so much mathematical garble without a computer to interpret and utilize it.

Functional
Solutions
Group

Functional
Solutions
Group

SOFTWARE THAT MAKES SENSE

P.O. Box 4198 • Laguna Beach • CA • 92652-4198 • 714.494.6155 • Fax 714.497.3927

After all the playing with the perfection of computer design, somebody remembered what it was like to have a hands-on look. Thus was born the computer backlash. The great irony dawns when we realize that design striving for a very uncomputerized look is designed on the computer. Grunge typefaces, special filters, tweaking options, and scanning are just some of the aids in this field which offers much artistic freedom to the designer.

creative firm: **ELLEN BRUSS DESIGN**
designers: **Ellen Bruss, Dae Ann Knight**
client: **BVP Media Inc.**

Illustrative styles and rough type suggest design touched by human hands.

creative firm: **FUZE**
designers: **Tom Sieu, Tim Carpenter**
client: **Christina Robbins Represents**

This stationery employs some very nice smudging and masking tape effects.

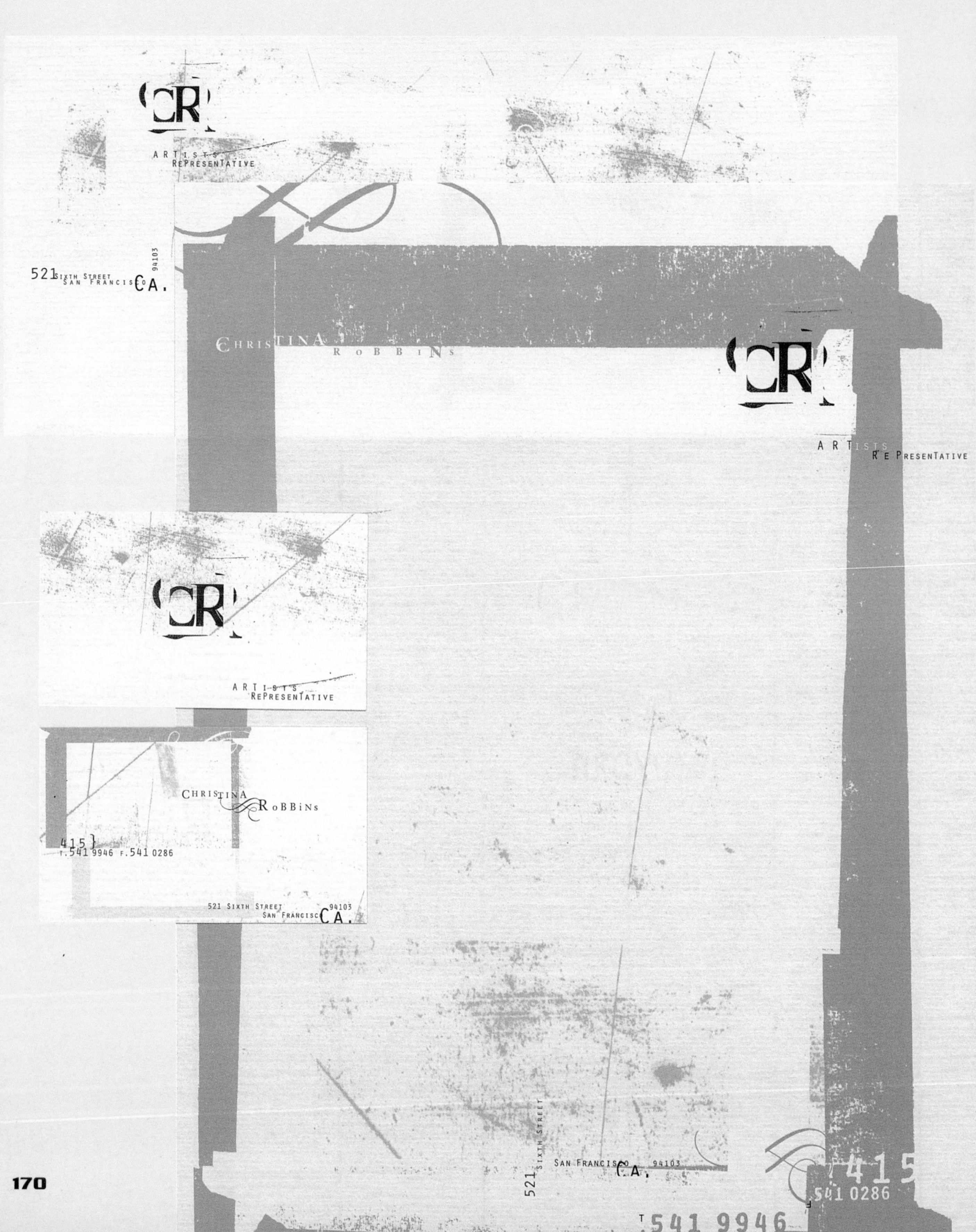

creative firm: **CROWLEY WEBB AND ASSOCIATES**
designer: **Brian Grunert**
client: **Buffalo Arts Studio**

An image can actually be created with paint (or whatever) and scanned in for computer use.

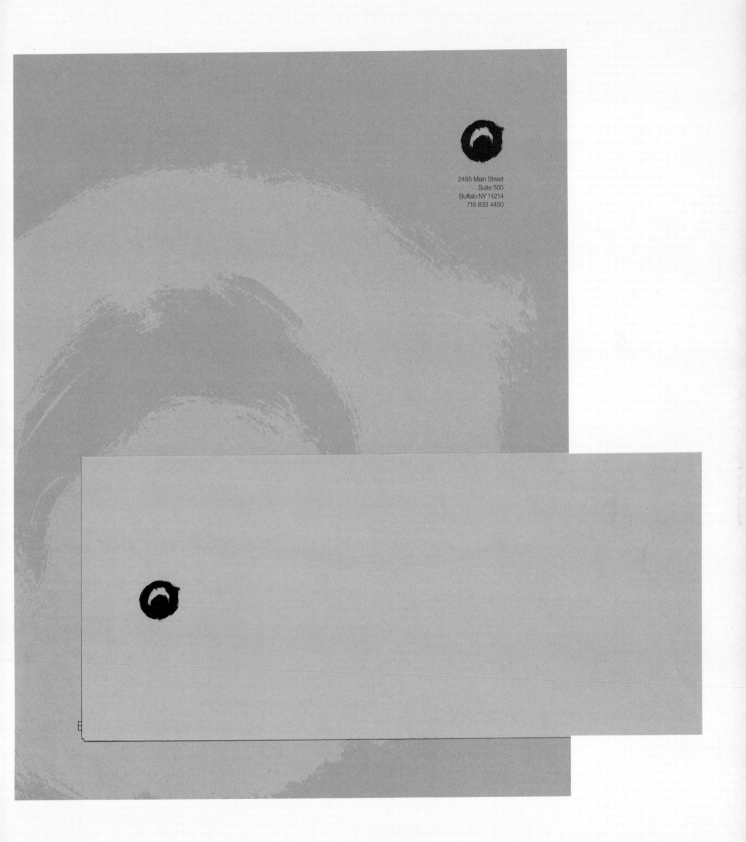

creative firm: TIEKEN DESIGN & CREATIVE SERVICES
designer: Fred E. Tieken
client: Tieken Design & Creative Services

Calligraphic effects can be produced in drawing programs or scanned in and used as artwork.

Tieken

TIEKEN
DESIGN
AND
CREATIVE
SERVICES
2800
NORTH
CENTRAL
AVENUE
SUITE
150
PHOENIX
ARIZONA
85004
TEL
602
230-0060
FAX
602
230-7574

TIEKEN
DESIGN
AND
CREATIVE
SERVICES
2800
NORTH
CENTRAL
AVENUE
SUITE
150
PHOENIX
ARIZONA
85004

Tieken

creative firm: HANDLER DESIGN GROUP, INC.
designer: Bruce Handler
client: Kydstuff, Inc.

Paint smudges can be drawn, tweaked, and colored for a realistic look.

Hand Painted Clothing
And Accessories
27 Sherwood Drive
Huntington NY 11743

Hand Painted Clothing
And Accessories
27 Sherwood Drive
Huntington NY 11743
516 367 4155
Kathy Diamond

Hand Painted Clothing
And Accessories
27 Sherwood Drive
Huntington NY 11743
516 367 4155
Kathy Diamond

creative firm: TACKETT-BARBARIA DESIGN
designer: Pam Matsuda
client: Chef's Market

Sketchy artwork creates a relaxed atmosphere.

Chef's Market Fine Foods

Davis California

the Marketplace
1411 Covell Boulevard, Suite 104 Davis, California 95616
phone 916.757.6880 fax 916.757.6879

Chef's Market

Fine Foods

Davis California

Chef's Market Fine Foods

Davis California

1411 Covell Boulevard, Suite 104
Davis, California 95616

JELKS CHEF'S MARKET, LIMITED LIABILITY COMPANY

creative firm: **A-HILL DESIGN**
designer: **Sandy Hill**
client: **Patricia Carlisle Fine Art Inc.**

A torn-paper look is incorporated into this initial logo.

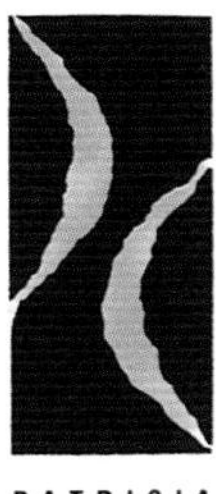

creative firm: WALL-TO-WALL STUDIOS
designers: Bernard Vy, James Nesbitt
client: The Cider People, Inc.

Woodcuts and hand stenciling are nice, crafted images.

THE CIDER PEOPLE, INC.
P.O. Box 14585, 1625 Central Parkway,
Cincinnati, OH 45250-0585

THE CIDER PEOPLE, INC.

Offices: P.O. Box 14585, 1625 Central Parkway, Cincinnati, OH 45250-0585
or P.O. Box 307, 627 Old Mill Road, Millersville, MD 21108
Tel:(513)721-2071 Fax:(513)721-2075 Web: http://www.cider-people.com/cider/

creative firm: **VISUAL ASYLUM**
designers: **Amy Levine, MaeLin Levine**
client: **Digigami**

Fonts with a calligraphic feel can really soften a company's image.

creative firm: **V N O DESIGN**
designer: **Jim Vienneau**
client: **Green Pastures Landscaping**

Rough illustrations reminiscent of scratchboard art can be readily executed on the computer

P O BOX 41791 NASHVILLE TENNESSEE 37204-1791

DAVID SHORE

P O BOX 41791 NASHVILLE TENNESSEE 37204-1791 TEL 615 255 3006

P O BOX 41791 NASHVILLE TENNESSEE 37204-1791 TEL 615 255 3006

creative firm: **WENDY QUESINBERRY DESIGN**
designer: **Wendy Quesinberry**
client: **Water Gardens**

Very freely rendered drawing and initial caps mesh well with more traditional fonts.

21810 SE 276th Street Maple Valley, WA 98038 Phone 425.413.7775 Fax 425.413.7361

creative firm: **STRONG PRODUCTIONS**
designers: **Todd Schatzberg, Matt Doty, Brian Cox**
client: **Dovetail Learning Systems**

The logo in this system has a very painterly feel, far removed from traditional computer work.

210 second street se
suite 200
cedar rapids, ia 52401

BRIAN DALZIEL
President and CEO
319.286.2999
210 second street se
suite 200
cedar rapids, ia 52401
sales: 1.888.713.3683
facsimile: 319.286.2988
email: bdalziel@inav.net

interactive multimedia
learning products:
cd-rom · internet · video

319.286.2999
sales: 1.888.713.3683
facsimile: 319.286.298

creative firm: **THE WELLER INSTITUTE FOR THE CURE OF DESIGN, INC.**
designer: **Don Weller**
client: **Dream Catcher Inn and Retreat**

A drawing that appears to be drawn with pen and ink can be produced in several different computer drawing programs.

DREAM

CATCHER
INN AND RETREAT

DREAM

CATCHER
INN AND RETREAT

191 South 200 East
Moab, Utah 84532

191 South 200 East
Moab, Utah 84532
1-888-230-3247
259-5998

creative firm: **SIEBERT DESIGN**
designer: **Lori Siebert**
client: **Scott Hull Associates**

Collages can be created on the computer where sizing images and pasting them up is no problem.

creative firm: **WILLOUGHBY DESIGN GROUP**
designer: Michelle Sonderegger
client: Willoughby Design Group

Signatures, rubber stamps, and illustrations can all be created via computer or scanned and used as artwork.

WILLOUGHBY DESIGN GROUP

WILLOUGHBY DESIGN GROUP
[602] Westport Road
Kansas City, MO 64111

WILLOUGHBY DESIGN GROUP
[602] Westport Road
Kansas City, MO 64111

WILLOUGHBY DESIGN GROUP
Ann Willoughby
Ann Willoughby
[602] Westport Road
Kansas City, MO 64111
Phone: 816. 561. 4189
Fax: 816. 561. 5052

AUG 0 1 1978

[602] Westport Road
Kansas City, MO 64111
Phone: 816. 561. 4189
Fax: 816. 561. 5052

AUG 0 1 1978

Index: Design **Firms**